ALL THIRTEEN

The Incredible Cave Rescue
of the Thai Boys' Soccer Team

ALL THIRTEEN

The Incredible Cave Rescue
of the Thai Boys' Soccer Team

CHRISTINA SOONTORNVAT

CANDLEWICK PRESS

First edition 2020

Library of Congress Catalog Card Number 2020918971
ISBN 978-1-5362-0945-7

21 22 23 24 25 LGO 10 9 8 7 6 5

Printed in Vicenza, Italy

This book was typeset in ITC Slimbach.

Candlewick Press
99 Dover Street
Somerville, Massachusetts 02144

www.candlewick.com

In memory of Saman Gunan, who gave his life to help others

And for my father, Amnaj Soontornvat

Contents

A soccer field at Mae Sai Prasitsart School, Mae Sai, Thailand

1.

A Typical Saturday

June 23, 2018

ON THE SOCCER FIELDS of Mae Sai, Thailand, it sounds like a typical Saturday morning:

The *tap-tap* of soccer balls passing cleat to cleat across the grass.

The *twee!* of the coach's whistle and shouts of "Mark up!" and "Make some space!"

The hard *thump* of a well-placed foot, followed by the best sound of all: silence as the ball flies past the goalie's fingertips, then a soft *swish* as it lands at the back of the net.

It's only practice for the Wild Boars, a local boys' team for players ages eleven to seventeen, but if they can keep sinking shots like that in their next game, they can't lose.

In Thailand, as in most of the world, soccer is not just a sport; it's a total obsession. The scuffle and shouts of pickup matches can be heard at all hours of the day, whether in an urban metropolis like Bangkok or here, in the small town of Mae Sai.

Practice finishes, and the boys huddle together, drinking water and wiping the sweat off their faces. It's a hot day, but at least there are clouds to shield them from the brutal sun. Talk shifts from World Cup rivalries to what they're going to do next. Everyone's eyes turn to twenty-five-year-old assistant coach Ekkapol Chantawong, whom everyone calls Coach Ek. He's been promising to take the team on an excursion to a local cave, and all the boys want to know if their outing is still on.

Being a Wild Boar means more than just getting together to play soccer a couple of times a week. The team is tight-knit, even though they go to different schools. The kids on the team have a reputation for being adventurous and outdoorsy, never sitting still for long, always ready to hop on their bikes to go exploring together. Coach Ek encourages the boys to be athletes beyond the soccer field, and he organizes regular hiking and bicycling expeditions for them. They often go swimming after practice, either at the neighborhood activity center or at local swimming holes. On the team's last outing — a strenuous bike ride to the top of a nearby mountain, Doi Tung — they discussed what their next trip would be. This area of Thailand is well known for its caves, the most famous of which is Tham Luang Nang Non — the Cave of the Sleeping Lady — and they had agreed to go there together.

Some teammates have to back out of the fun. They have too much homework, or their parents have made them promise to come home for this reason or that. But twelve of the boys are still up for the adventure.

Night reminds the team that it's his birthday. His parents are having a party that evening, complete with food, a big cake, and lots of friends and family. The team is invited, too, but they can't show up late, and they definitely can't show up covered in cave mud.

Coach Ek tells them, "We have to be out by five o'clock."

Everyone agrees. They'll go for only an hour or so, and then they'll head back.

The boys buy snacks to top up their energy before the bike ride to the cave. They go for the good stuff: junk food, like chips, soda, and

The Boys of the Wild Boars

In Thailand, everyone has a formal first name and last name that are usually reserved for official occasions. Friends and family tend to call one another by a short one- or two-syllable nickname. People also address each other with a word that describes how they are related. For example, brothers and sisters call each other Pi (for older siblings) or Nong (for younger siblings). But even people who are not related by blood will use these terms as a sign of respect and affection. The Wild Boars all call each other "Brother," and they refer to their coach as "Coach Ek" or "Big Brother Ek."

Members of the Wild Boars soccer team. Boys' nicknames and ages at the time of entering the cave (left to right, back row): Note (14), Night (16), Thi (16), Tern (14), former Manchester United Football Team player Gary Pallister, Mix (13), Coach Ek (25), Nick (15). (Left to right, front row): Adul (14), Titan (11), Mark (13), Pong (13), Dom (13), Bew (14).

This Is Mae Sai

The boys' home base of Mae Sai is a small but bustling town on Thailand's northern border. Market carts display all sorts of wares from Thailand, Myanmar, Laos, China, and beyond. Goods flow back and forth across the border. People too. Mae Sai is as diverse as you'd expect a border town to be. In the markets, you hear Thai spoken alongside Lao, Mandarin, Cantonese, Burmese (the official language of Myanmar), and local indigenous languages. Tourists come here from all over the world, but especially from China, Europe, and the United States. Most people in Mae Sai are Buddhist, but Muslims and Christians also call the town home. It's a vibrant, busy place, where women balance baskets of coffee beans on their shoulders as motorbikes zip in and out of the lanes of traffic, waiting their turn to cross the border.

In this region, most families are farmers or members of the working class. The Wild Boars know that getting a good education is vital. They hope that if they study hard and get a good job someday, they can earn enough money to help support their families. Maybe then they can give something back to their parents, who work tirelessly so their children can focus on school and soccer.

their favorite candy bar, called Beng-Beng. And they scarf it down before setting out.

They laugh and call out to each other as they cycle along. The oldest boys — Thi, Night, and Night's cousin Nick — are good friends with the coach. Fourteen-year-old Adul is quite close to Coach Ek, too. Adul is the only non-Buddhist in the group, and he is devoted to the Christian church he attends in Mae Sai, where he sings and plays guitar. The other parishioners raised money to send him to a good local school, where he is at the top of all his classes.

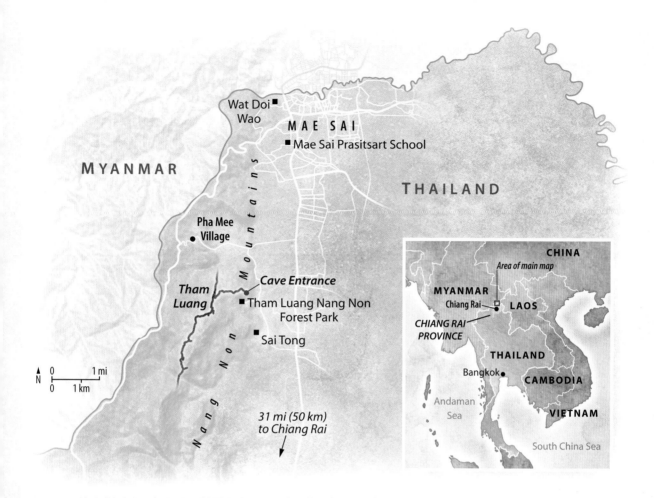

Pedaling with him are fellow eighth-graders Note and Tern. Bew weaves among his friends, driving his moped. Next come the inseparable thirteen-year-olds, who go to school together: Dom, who is the team captain; Mix; and Pong, a jokester who isn't as serious about class as the other boys. The "little" boys work to keep up: thirteen-year-old Mark, who is the smallest member on the team, and eleven-year-old, chubby-cheeked Titan, the youngest player, who begged his parents to let him join the Wild Boars. Despite the differences in their ages, these twelve boys are very good friends. They hardly ever get into arguments, though

The entrance to Tham Luang–Khun Nam Nang Non Forest Park

they do love to tease little Titan, who usually takes it all in stride with his big smile.

As the boys cycle on, paved roads give way to dirt, and neighborhood dogs trot out to greet them. The Nang Non mountain range rises up behind them, a blurry dark green, as they ride past homes and apartments, repair shops, and open-front stores selling furniture, restaurant equipment, and plastic toys.

After a few minutes on their bikes, the boys are on the one-lane roads that wind through farms and into the mountains. The Wild Boars love these trips, when they can leave behind their stacks of homework and get up into the fresh green hills that hover over their neighborhoods.

The boys' parents are happy that their children are adventurous. It's much better for them to be out in nature, exercising their bodies and minds, than stuck at home watching a screen or wandering under the artificial lights of a shopping mall. Besides, they're with Coach Ek, who is much more than just a coach.

Ek believes that his duties don't end on the field. He feels that in order to be a good leader, he needs to understand the boys as individuals. In turn, they sometimes listen to their coach more than they do their own parents. But rather than being annoyed, the parents are grateful that their sons have such a good influence. They trust Ek deeply, and he even baby-sits for them sometimes. He is young enough to feel like another son or nephew to the boys' families, but he carries the wisdom and maturity of someone who has been through too many of life's hardships. They hope their sons can learn to be like him. Luckily, the boys want the same thing.

Tham Luang is only a few miles from the soccer field, and the team turns off the main road after about half an hour. As they pump up the gravelly track to the entrance, birds swoop through groves of banana and lychee trees. Yellow-and-brown-spotted butterflies flit past as pineapple fields give way to thick jungle that shades the road. The last bit of the bike ride is all uphill: muggy and sweaty. Soon the team is gratefully walking their bikes toward the cool, dark mouth of the cave. They set their bikes on the ground outside and swap their cleats for flip-flops. Coach Ek leads the boys up to the entrance, bringing along the supplies he's packed: a coil of thin rope and flashlights. They walk past a faded sign warning visitors not to enter during the rainy season, as the cave floods at that time.

But they don't pay the sign much attention. It's only June 23, and the heavy rains are still weeks away.

Clouds hover over the Nang Non mountain range.

2.
A Sky Full of Water

June 23, 2018

THE PARK RANGERS who work at Tham Luang Nang Non Forest Park have a light day on June 23. During busy times, they lead tours into the cave, guiding people into the impressive entrance chambers and giving talks about how the structures have formed. But now that the high season for tourists has passed, Tham Luang will see only a handful of visitors, taking selfies or paying their respects to the shrine at the cave entrance.

Pretty soon, visitors to Tham Luang will stop completely. Monsoon season officially started in May, but the steady, heavy rains come in July.

Thailand has three seasons: hot, cool, and rainy (also called monsoon season). Here in Southeast Asia, the monsoon rains can be torrential. In the summer, as the sun heats the land, moist air blows in from the ocean and settles over the continent. In northern Thailand, the clouds will gather, full and low around the mountains, where they will hover for the whole season. Most days, in the afternoon or evening, the clouds will crack open and the rain will fall. In just a few months, the skies will dump 90 percent of the year's rainfall. Walking outside in this type of rain can feel like walking through a waterfall. The water barrels down in thick sheets, making umbrellas and raincoats almost useless. And it falls and falls for months. In town, streets and alleys become little canals as all that rain drains downhill.

The monsoon brings the waters of life. The mountains glow green through the gray deluge. The rains run down through the lush forests, carrying nutrients into the surrounding farmland, making the soil rich and ripe for growing crops. As soon as the rains stop, the fields will burst with bounty: coffee, fruit, vegetables, and acres of rice. This area, once its own kingdom, is called Lanna, the Land of a Million Rice Fields.

The rainy season is usually predictable. People who live in low areas build their houses up on stilts, and anyone living close to a river or stream builds their home far away from the banks, knowing how they can flood. But even with preparation, floods can overwhelm whole towns, trapping people in their homes, washing away roads, and causing deadly landslides in the mountains.

A changing climate has been making the seasons less predictable. The warming planet has warmed the air, too. Warmer air can hold more moisture, making wet areas wetter and dry areas drier. All over southern Asia, rainfalls have become more extreme.

In the days leading up to June 23, the area around Tham Luang cave has had some unusually high rain. And it looks as though it's in for more. The clouds that have hung over the mountain all day drop lower and lower.

The rain begins beating down.

ALL THIRTEEN

Crop fields at the foot of the Nang Non mountains

The Nang Non mountains form the outline of the Sleeping Lady's face and body.

3.

The Cave of the Sleeping Lady

June 23, 2018

COACH EK LEADS THE TWELVE MEMBERS of his team up the steps to the mouth of Tham Luang. On the way, they stop to bow and pay their respects at a shrine to Jao Mae Nang Non, the Sleeping Lady. She is said to have been an ancient princess who fell in love with a servant. Knowing her father, the king, would never approve, she ran away with her lover, and the two of them hid inside the cave. But when the servant went out to look for food, he was captured and killed by the king's soldiers. The heartbroken princess killed herself. Her blood became the water flowing in the cave, and her body became the mountain. If you look at the Nang Non mountain range at the right angle, you can see the outline of her face and body.

For many of the people of northern Thailand, caves are particularly sacred places that deserve respect. In the ancient stories, these caves are homes to monsters who have lured in princes. They house giants who were defeated by the Buddha himself. Some caves contain entire temples inside them, and Buddhist monks have been known to spend years

Steps leading up to the cave entrance

The entrance into Tham Luang

meditating in the darkness within. A mountain holds power, and a cave provides a way to tap into that power. But as the story of the Sleeping Lady shows, that power can be both enticing and dangerous.

As the boys step inside Tham Luang's impressive entrance chamber, they breathe in the damp air and the smell of wet, mossy limestone. The ceiling soars to about 100 feet, more than 30 meters, and the whole chamber is big enough to hold a 747 jet. Thick stalactite spires hang down like dragon teeth. Over thousands of years, water that dripped down from the ceiling left behind tiny deposits of calcium minerals that hardened into the sparkling formations. When the dripping water lands on the cave floor, it can also build a stack of minerals that grows from the ground up, called a stalagmite. When a stalactite and a stalagmite meet, they can form a column or even a flowing curtain of shiny stone.

The Wild Boars gaze up at the slick cave walls. Twenty feet (six meters) up, a dark line of mud marks the highest level of the last flood. The floor of the cavern is dry and packed down by heavy foot traffic.

The first 2,000 feet (600 meters) of the Tham Luang cave system are made up of big, airy rooms like the entrance chamber. Beyond this point, the cave narrows. Some sections force visitors into a crouch and then a crawl, where the ceiling drops to just a few feet high. Here, cavers are well beyond the "twilight zone," the part of the cave where light from the outside world still reaches. Without a flashlight the darkness is complete. If you are claustrophobic, this is where you turn around.

But the boys aren't deterred by the tight spaces, and there are no barriers, gates, or ropes to stop them from continuing on. The cave winds along, down steep and slippery sections. About one mile in, the route makes a sharp hairpin turn and dumps into a three-way junction called Sam Yaek.

From where the boys stand, the right-hand path leads to a lesser-explored stretch known as the Monk's Series. On the left, an opening low in the wall leads to the main cave. In caving lingo, the phrase "it goes" means that a passage continues on, without a dead end. To the left, Tham

THAM LUANG CAVE SYSTEM WITH CROSS SECTIONS

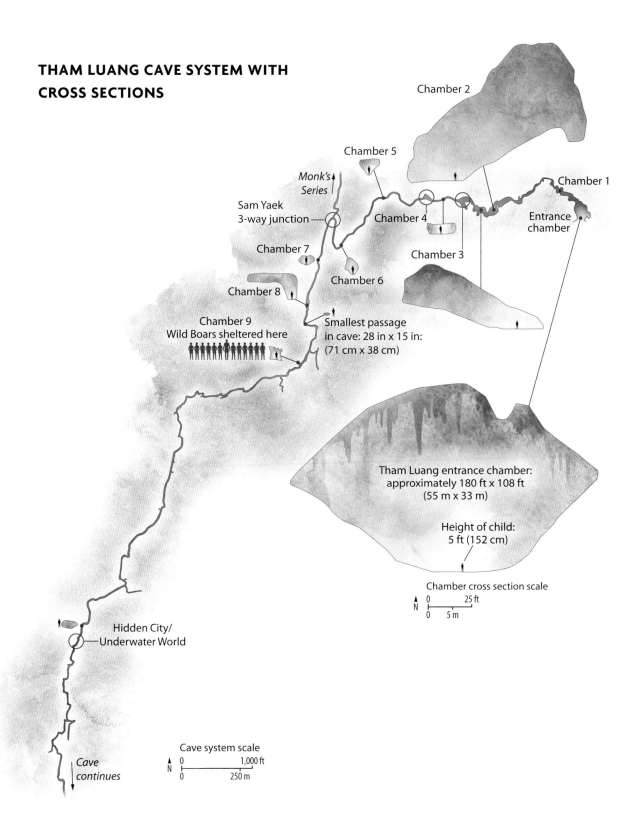

Chamber 2

Chamber 5

Chamber 1

Monk's
Series

Sam Yaek
3-way junction

Chamber 4

Entrance
chamber

Chamber 7

Chamber 3

Chamber 6

Chamber 8

Chamber 9
Wild Boars sheltered here

Smallest passage
in cave: 28 in x 15 in:
(71 cm x 38 cm)

Tham Luang entrance chamber:
approximately 180 ft x 108 ft
(55 m x 33 m)

Height of child:
5 ft (152 cm)

Chamber cross section scale

N 0   25 ft
   0   5 m

Hidden City/
Underwater World

Cave system scale

N 0   1,000 ft
   0   250 m

Cave
continues

Luang "goes," and it goes quite far. The most recent survey measures the known end of the cave system to be almost seven miles, or 11 kilometers, away from the entrance.

At first the Wild Boars have no intention of going nearly that far. They've already spent more than their one hour of time and really should be turning back. But now that they're here, deep into the cave, they fall into the allure that all cavers know well: *What if we go just a little farther?*

At Sam Yaek, they kick off their shoes, drop their backpacks, and head left.

Past the junction, Tham Luang pitches its visitors into more tight squeezes. Even without claustrophobia, you might get uneasy when the walls close in tight enough to force you to slither forward on your belly. You might feel out of your element here, thinking of all the miles of rock both above and beneath. Maybe you imagine getting trapped, being buried under millions of tons of stone. It's not a pleasant feeling when you still have miles of passage between you and the exit.

Or maybe you are someone who views being inside a cave quite differently. A cave is one of the most serene places you can go. It's no wonder that Buddhist monks have been known to seek out caves for long meditations. It is cool and fairly quiet. Without all the distractions that surround you aboveground, you can focus on the small things that you usually never notice, like the soft echo of your breath against the rocks.

And yet a cave is not sterile. A cave has a life of its own. In Tham Luang, if you hold quite still, you can feel it "breathing," a light whisper of air flowing through the system. Maybe being this deep in the earth gives you the same perspective as astronauts floating high above it: a sense that you are a very tiny part of a very large universe.

The boys wriggle through tight spaces that cavers call squeezes and boulder chokes, where stones that fell from the ceiling long ago have clogged up the passages. They tromp up and down sandy, gravelly slopes. Their bare toes, toughened by years of shoeless soccer matches, grip the slippery rocks as they climb through sections that dip steeply down before pitching back up again. Suddenly, they come upon a pool of water.

Coach Ek pauses.

He has been in Tham Luang before, and he knows that the cave can hold pockets of water along the route, so he isn't concerned. However, Coach Ek is the type of leader who doesn't like to order other people around. Instead, he likes for the group to make decisions together. He wants every boy to feel as though he has a voice. When they come upon the water, he asks if the boys want to keep going.

Sixteen-year-old Thi offers to check how deep the water is. The rest of the team watches as he wades down into the pool and pushes off. Soon Thi is smiling on the other side.

"Come on. You can all follow me!" he calls back to them. His toes touched the bottom the whole way. The water's a little cold, but they can definitely make it.

The rest of the team follows, with the bigger boys carrying the little ones on their backs.

It isn't long before that gentle whisper of air they have felt throughout the cave becomes a roar. A sharp draft of wind sends a sudden spray of water droplets onto their faces, startling them. But Coach Ek knows where they are and leads them on.

They have reached a room that locals call Hidden City or Underwater World. Here, the roof lowers over a pool that exists year-round, even in the dry season. The water level of the pool is high right now, which pinches the airflow, making it gust faster. Even with the roaring wind, the room is lovely, in an eerie, haunting sort of way. Names of past adventurers who have reached this point are scrawled into the walls.

Tham Luang still goes, though few people other than the most dedicated explorers have ever made it past this point. Hardly anyone ever gets this far in the first place. It's a huge accomplishment, especially since some of the boys haven't even been inside the cave before. The boys have hiked in almost three miles, or five kilometers, and they have done most of it barefoot. In a moment like this, you have to stop and soak it all in.

Coach Ek says that the cave keeps going beyond the pool. But if they want to see it, they'll have to get wet again, and this time they'll have to dunk their heads under. Do the boys want to go? Or should they head back?

Thi, the only one on the team wearing a watch, tells the others what time it is. They have spent almost three hours inside already. If they want to be out of the cave in time for Night to make his party, they are going to have to absolutely fly back home. They decide to turn around.

Everyone scrambles and squirms back toward the entrance. They swim back across the water they crossed on their way in. They hustle forward in single file, trying to go as quickly as possible without twisting an ankle on the slippery rocks.

And then Coach Ek hears Bew, who is up at the front of the group, call back to him.

"Coach, come see! There's water here!"

Coach squeezes past the others to the front of the line.

"Hey, are we lost?" one of the boys behind him asks. "Did we take a wrong turn?"

"No," Coach Ek assures them. "We can't be lost. There's only one way out, for sure."

The boys point to the source of their confusion. They should be approaching Sam Yaek, the three-way junction, but now there is a pool of swirling water that wasn't there before.

The water completely blocks the way forward. The passage they came through is somewhere under the turbulent water, but they can't see it.

Tham Luang is flooding.

The boys' bikes outside the cave

4.

First on the Scene

June 23, 2018

NIGHT misses his birthday party.

His family grows worried as the evening goes on and he still doesn't show up. Calls are made among family members, who then call friends and teammates. None of the boys had told their parents where they were going. The parents soon learn that their sons had messaged other members of the team to tell them of their plans to go to Tham Luang.

Now the families' worry turns to real fear.

At 9:45 p.m. on Saturday, June 23, Sangwut Khammongkhon, the director of the Siam Ruam Jai Mae Sai Rescue Organization, takes a phone call from the village chief near Tham Luang, who tells him that a team of soccer players has gone missing and relatives suspect that the children are trapped in the cave. Sangwut is not surprised as he listens to the details. He has taken calls like this before about Tham Luang, when tourists or hikers have been stuck in the caverns. A dropped flashlight or a dead battery is usually to blame, and it doesn't take long to find the missing

Rescuer Sangwut Khammongkhon

people. Sangwut follows his rescue protocol, grabbing ropes, flashlights, and first-aid supplies, and loads up his truck in the rain.

By the time Sangwut hits the highway, rain lashes his windshield. It's coming down hard now, and he takes the turn into the park cautiously. When he pulls up to the parking lot, he sees that some of the parents have already gathered near the mouth of the cave. Sangwut climbs out of his truck and assures the families that everything will be fine. He has already called the other members of his organization, and soon the eighteen-person rescue team has set up floodlights in the entrance chamber.

The boys' bikes have been moved from where they were left on the ground, and now they lean against the railing at the entrance, with soccer cleats lying at the tires. Sangwut isn't sure that the boys are actually inside the cave; they could have been exploring somewhere else in the area. But with rain coming down in torrents, he gets an itching worry in the back of his mind. Before he goes into the cave, he makes a call to the Sirikorn Rescue Association, in the nearby city of Chiang Rai, and asks them to come to Tham Luang. Sirikorn has special equipment that Sangwut's team lacks: scuba-diving gear.

Sangwut leads his team into Tham Luang. Despite the heavy rains pummeling the mountain outside, the first chambers of the cave are completely dry. An hour and a half later, Sangwut's team arrives at Sam Yaek, the bowl-shaped chamber where the three main branches of the cave meet. To their left and lower down, a passage leads southwest.

At least, it usually does.

Sam Yaek is full of water. The left-hand passage sits low in the chamber, and water that has pooled in the bottom of the junction has covered up the opening completely.

Even more discouraging, Sangwut finds footprints and sees a pile of backpacks and sandals near the junction. He cups his hands around his mouth and shouts for the children. He calls up into Monk's Series as loud as he can, but he hears nothing back. With a sinking feeling in his stomach, Sangwut understands that the team must have gone left and are now trapped by the water pooled over the opening to the passageway.

The Sirikorn rescue specialists arrive at Tham Luang and enter the cave at 1:00 a.m. Twenty-two rescue workers, park staff, and even some Royal Thai Army soldiers who were in the area carry ropes and air canisters into the cave, back to Sam Yaek. At the junction, Sirikorn's divers strap on their equipment. With no wet suits, the cold water is a shock as they sink in and begin to look for the left-hand opening. They surface and dive again and again in the swirling water and finally manage to locate the hole through the muddy murk. But the opening is too small. The divers' bulky air tanks, mounted on their backs, ram against the top of the passage.

The Sirikorn divers use scuba gear for recovering bodies from the bottom of lakes or rivers, not for diving through flooded caves. The divers aren't equipped to make it through the narrow passage. They decide to halt the diving and hike back out to the cave entrance to talk through a plan.

When they emerge into the open air at 4:00 a.m., Sangwut is surprised to see that the number of family members waiting outside has

The boys' worried family members gather at the cave.

multiplied. When the families see the rescue workers come out — with no children in tow — they are furious.

"What are you doing?" they shout. "How can you stop searching now?"

Some of the boys' cousins who have been inside the cave many times try to barge past the rescue workers. "We know the way!" they say. They are ready to pull the boys out themselves, if that's what it takes.

The boys' mothers and fathers call into the cave. Their voices crack with anguish. "My son, I'm here! Come home! I'm waiting for you!"

Sangwut's heart breaks to hear them, and he understands their frustration. He calms the families, but he doesn't tell them about the water at Sam Yaek junction. He doesn't want them to panic. Instead, he tells them that the team has come out of the cave because it's so late, and they will resume the search first thing in the morning. The families grudgingly accept this explanation, but they do not leave the scene.

The governor of Chiang Rai province, Narongsak Osatanakorn, has arrived on-site. He calls a meeting for all the rescue workers in one of the park headquarters buildings. They agree to pause the rescue because it's too dangerous to dive without proper equipment. They also agree that they must shut down the cave. No one can go in or out without passing a checkpoint. The last step they agree to will fall on the governor's shoulders to carry out: they must tell the parents that their children have been trapped by floodwaters inside. Even though the families are sure to panic, they need to know the truth.

Sangwut leaves the meeting, the heavy clouds over his heart matching those in the sky. He knows this cave very well. And he knows that when water reaches Sam Yaek at this time of the year, it doesn't go down until after the rainy season is over.

That night Sangwut knows they are in for a long, long rescue.

Rescue workers in the entrance chamber of Tham Luang

A creek flows with water that has drained off the Nang Non mountains.

5.
Trapped

June 23, 2018

THE WILD BOARS are only about a mile from the cave entrance, about an hour-and-a-half hike from their bikes. They look down at the water pooling at their feet where there had previously been dry ground. It is as cloudy as a cup of milky coffee. They can't see the forward passage at all, but they know it's there.

Coach Ek wonders how bad the flooding is. If the flooded section isn't too long, maybe they could manage to swim out. He will give it a try first.

Coach Ek unspools the coil of rope he brought with them. He ties one end around his waist and hands the other end to Thi, Night, and Adul.

As he wades into the water, he gives them instructions. "Once I swim in, if I can't find any way forward, I'll tug the rope twice and you'll pull me back. But if I don't tug on the rope at all, you'll know we can make it through, and you can swim in after me."

The boys nod and grip tight to the rope. Their heartbeats race as they watch their coach take a deep breath and plunge into the water.

The cold current swirls around Coach Ek. It's strong, and it pushes him back toward the boys waiting behind him. They shine their flashlights into the water to give him some light. But even with his eyes wide open, he can't see through the dirty swill. He swims forward for a few strokes, stretching his feet down to check if he can reach the bottom. His toes kick sand. He reaches overhead. The water goes all the way to the rock above. There is no air space at all.

What if this flooded section is just a short duck under? Maybe the surface is only a few feet away. Maybe he can reach it. But his air is running out. If he goes any farther, he might not have enough air in his lungs to make it back. Even if he does make it to the other side, it's doubtful that the boys can get through. And what if he is unable to swim back to help them?

Quickly, he yanks the rope twice. He feels the tug of the boys on the other end. He kicks his legs as they reel him in.

Coach Ek gets out of the water, dripping and chilled. He knows that if he uses the word "trapped," the boys could panic. He stays calm and explains that they won't be able to get out this way with the water so high. But if they wait, it will go down, and then they'll be able to swim out.

The boys look at one another. They don't understand. They just came this way. How could the water have risen so quickly?

In order to understand how the Wild Boars became suddenly stranded inside the cave, you have to understand more about the cave itself. Tham Luang is the fourth longest cave in Thailand. Compared to the longest known cave in the world, Mammoth Cave, in Kentucky, which is 405 miles (653 kilometers) long, the Cave of the Sleeping Lady is just a baby. But it's not the cave's length that makes it dangerous.

It's the way it floods.

The mountain that holds Tham Luang cave is made of rock called karst limestone. This is a very holey type of rock found all over the world,

Karst formations in Halong Bay, Vietnam

from Southeast Asia to the United States. Wherever you find karst, you almost always find caves.

When rain falls on the Nang Non mountains, it doesn't just run over the surface. Much of that rain sinks straight down into the mountain's millions of holes, soaking into the ground like a sponge. When the Wild Boars walked into Tham Luang, it was dry. But what the boys didn't realize was that the heavy rains that hit the area a few days before had completely saturated the ground beneath their feet. The boys didn't know that the dry ground they walked on masked a mountain already filled to the brim with water.

Any extra water — like the rain that started to fall after the boys went inside — has nowhere else to go, so it flows through the cave itself. And it flows fast. Karst caves are known to flash flood in an instant. The network of tunnels in a karst mountain is like an underground river system. Tiny passages near the surface carry rainwater deeper into the mountain, where the passages widen and join bigger streams, which connect to even bigger streams. In some cave systems, entire raging rivers of water gush through the rock, putting white-water rapids to shame.

A Cave Is Born

Like all limestone, Thailand's karst began with dead marine creatures. Around 250 to 500 million years ago, the surface of Thailand actually sat beneath a sea teeming with animal life. Corals, clams, sea fans, and millions of other species lived in the sea. When they died, they sank to the bottom. Their bodies decomposed, but a mineral in their shells and skeletons, called calcium carbonate, remained. The calcium carbonate combined with mud on the seafloor as more and more remains of dead organisms continued to float down. Over millions of years, the pressure of the ocean sitting on top gradually pressed all those layers of calcium carbonate into limestone.

Our seemingly solid Earth is actually in constant evolution. The planet's crust is made of continental plates that float on layers of flowing magma. The Indian continental plate is sliding underneath the continent of Asia, forcing it up. Over millions of years, that lifting action eventually raised the limestone of Thailand higher and higher, until what was once the bottom of the sea became the top of the mountains. Up on the mountain, that limestone was then exposed to the climate, including rain. And a tropical area like Thailand gets lots and lots of rain.

Rainwater is slightly acidic. When it falls on a forest and flows through decaying leaves on the forest floor, it becomes even more acidic. Acid dissolves calcium carbonate in the limestone, forming a new type of landscape called karst.

If you were to drop a limestone rock in a glass of white vinegar, you'd see fizzing and bubbling as the acid in the vinegar dissolved the calcium carbonate in the rock. Picture the same thing happening to the limestone mountains of northern Thailand — only much slower and over millions of years — and you can imagine how caves like Tham Luang were formed. As water dissolved holes into the karst, the slope of the mountain and the cracks in the stone allowed the water to flow from one hole to another. With enough time and enough water, long tunnels and huge rooms formed deep underground.

A KARST CAVE SYSTEM

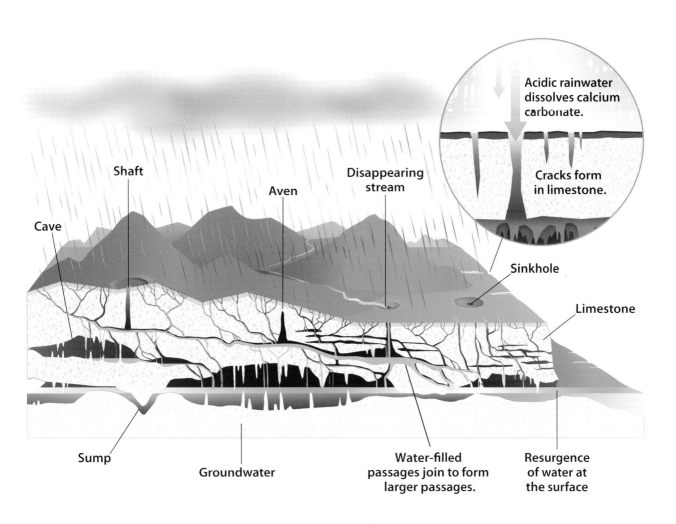

Acidic rainwater dissolves calcium carbonate.

Cracks form in limestone.

Shaft

Aven

Disappearing stream

Cave

Sinkhole

Limestone

Sump

Groundwater

Water-filled passages join to form larger passages.

Resurgence of water at the surface

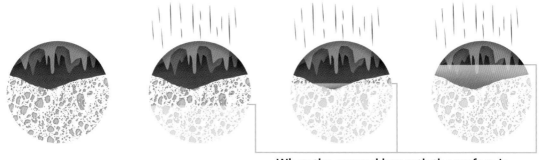

When the ground beneath the surface is completely saturated with water, continued rainfall can cause flooding.

Trapped as they are, the situation for the Wild Boars could be even worse. Tham Luang has only partially flooded for now. The rains outside have not created a deluge inside the mountain.

Not yet.

At 5:00 p.m. on Saturday, the boys are more afraid of their parents than of the cave. None of the boys told their families where they were going. Mark realizes how late it will be by the time he gets home and worries about the scolding he'll get once he does show up. Thi knows his mom is going to be furious. Some of the boys start thinking about all the homework they have to do for school.

Coach Ek wonders if they can dig a canal for the water to flow into. Maybe if they dig it deep enough, that will allow the water to subside and make enough space for them to swim through. The boys grab rocks and start digging in the gravelly dirt. They dig and dig, but it quickly becomes clear that they're not making any change in the water levels.

Suddenly everyone is exhausted. It isn't late, but the rush of adrenaline from realizing they are trapped has now worn off, and fatigue hits them like a truck.

Thi checks his watch again. It's 6:00 p.m. now. "Coach, do you think we should find someplace to sleep?"

The boys all agree that they should rest and wait for the water to go down. Coach Ek leads the way deeper into the cave to a section where the ground is sandy and water drips from the rocks along the cave walls.

Night thinks about his party and all the friends and family invited. He thinks about the food he knows his mother has been cooking all afternoon, and the cake.

His teammates are thinking of food, too. It's useless, though, unless they want to eat flashlights for dinner. They have no food with them. The only snacks they had were eaten before they entered the cave. Luckily, they do have the most important thing their bodies need — water.

Coach tells them that drinking the murky water from the pools on the cave floor isn't safe. It could have run straight over the ground and into the cave, carrying all sorts of harmful bacteria. But the water dripping from the walls has probably filtered down more slowly through the rocks overhead, cleaning it somewhat.

The boys drink the water as best they can, cupping their hands to catch the drops as they fall. It tastes good and clean, like spring water.

They find the driest spots they can and lie down together. Coach knows that he needs to keep calm and positive so that no one gets upset. Luckily everyone seems all right. Other than worrying about being in trouble with their parents, none of the boys are panicking. Before they go to sleep, he tells them all to pray together, just as they would before going to bed at home.

When the prayers are finished, Coach Ek tells them not to worry; the water will go down, and the parks department staff will be looking for them. One by one, the boys drift off to sleep, thinking about tomorrow, when they'll be able to get out.

Caver Vern Unsworth maneuvers through a squeeze in Tham Luang.

6.

The Cave Man

June 24–25, 2018

SANGWUT AND THE OTHER LOCAL RESCUERS who have gathered at Tham Luang agree that they need to call in someone who knows the cave better than anyone else. Vernon "Vern" Unsworth is a British caver who moved to Mae Sai seven years ago to be with his partner, Woranan "Tik" Ratrawiphakkun. Like many visitors to northern Thailand, Vern fell in love with the place: the beautiful mountains, the kindhearted people, and—best of all—the cave. Vern began caving as a teenager in the hills around his home in England, and forty years later, he is still obsessed with caves.

Like most explorers, cavers are motivated by the thrill of the unknown. But unlike a mountain climber, who can look up and see the peak that they will attempt to climb, cavers have no idea what awaits them beyond the beam of their flashlight. It may be a tight squeeze, or it may be a gaping chamber dripping with stalactites, as beautiful and awe-inspiring as any cathedral built by humans. The experience of setting foot in a passage that has never been reached by any other human is indescribable.

Some cavers call this experience "scooping booty," as though they are pirates digging their hands through trunks full of treasure. Beyond the big entrance chambers that attract tourists, Tham Luang still offers plenty of treasure to scoop.

Vern has a passion for mapping the cave's twisting routes and finding out where passages join up with other tunnels. It's like putting together a giant underground puzzle. Earlier in the year, he and his good friend Rob Harper completed an updated survey, or map, of the cave's farthest extensions. Vern has led many Thai friends into Tham Luang, guiding them as far as they are willing to venture. Mae Sai is a pretty small place where everyone knows everyone else, so even people who have never been to Tham Luang before know Vern as the Cave Man. It's no surprise that the rescue team calls him that very night.

In a lucky coincidence, Vern is already packed and ready to go. He had planned to visit Tham Luang the same day the boys went missing, but he ended up getting delayed. As he makes the drive to the park entrance, he has the troubling thought that if he had gone ahead with his original plan, he might have been trapped inside the cave himself. The boys have had an extraordinary twist of bad luck.

Vern pulls up to the cave around 6:30 a.m. on the day after the boys were trapped. He makes the hike down to the Sam Yaek junction and is surprised to see so much water there. Water is now pouring out of Monk's Series into the chamber. Vern knows, of course, that Tham Luang floods. Every year, water fills the system, reaching all the way out to Chamber 1. But last year, in 2017, the floodwaters didn't start coming until July 15. This is three weeks too early.

Rescue workers ask Vern if he thinks the team could have gone right, up into Monk's Series. Vern says it's highly unlikely. That passage is, in his words, "not nice," which is putting it mildly. Monk's Series is hundreds of yards of cramped, muddy crawling through passages so tight and sharp they leave you scraped and bruised. Even a small man like Vern has long scars along his back from trying to squish his body into those

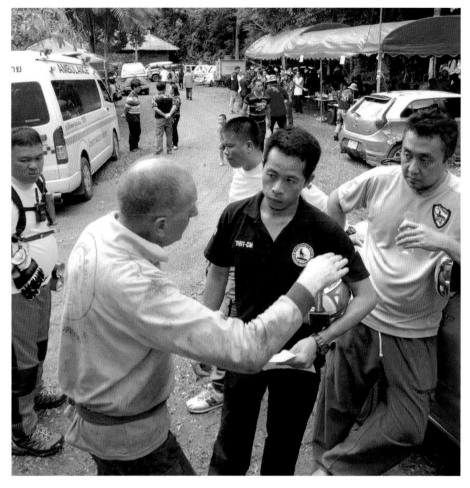

Vern Unsworth (left) speaking with local rescuers at Tham Luang base camp

passages. For a team of boys out for a fun adventure, that would not be the way to go.

It's much more likely that they went left. Based on the elevations that he has surveyed, Vern guesses that they could be sheltering on higher ground about a third of a mile (half a kilometer) past Sam Yaek. The bowl-shaped room of Sam Yaek is lower than other parts of the cave, so while the junction is filled with water, there are still chambers that are high enough to provide a dry harbor for the team.

The interior of Tham Luang

Cell phones are useless inside the cave, so in order to report any information to the rescue team outside, Vern, who is sixty-three, has to hike out and give it to them himself. This day, he makes the round-trip journey to the water-filled junction and back five separate times, a total distance of about 12 miles, or 20 kilometers.

Workers carry sandbags inside to try to stop the flow coming in from Monk's Series, but so much water is rushing in that the sandbags do nothing. It's clear that in order to reach the children, they need people who can dive through the flooded passage.

Local press has arrived to report on the growing story. "These kids are athletes," the deputy governor assures reporters. "They are alert and always active. They will try to survive by continuing to move."

The Wild Boars' head coach (and Coach Ek's supervisor), Nopparat Kanthawong, has been waiting anxiously with the boys' families outside the cave. "I believe up until this very moment that my team members and my assistant coach still have some light left. They will not abandon each other," says Coach Nopparat.

The boys' families are emotionally drained. It's now Monday morning, and they haven't left Tham Luang since arriving Saturday evening. "I haven't slept," says Mark's mom, who keeps fainting from the stress. "My son is a strong boy," she insists. "I still have hope." Relatives and family friends hold vigil outside the cave. They murmur prayer after prayer in front of a shrine adorned with flowers and images of the Buddha.

Hope finally arrives in the wee hours of Monday morning, as a team of twenty Royal Thai Navy SEALs land at the Chiang Rai airport with diving gear in tow.

The SEALs are the country's elite special operations unit. Their training is modeled on the United States Navy SEAL program. SEAL is an acronym for Sea, Air, and Land, and these teams are often deployed in highly dangerous, highly secretive operations, such as capturing pirates along

Shoes found inside Tham Luang

The Thai Navy SEALs arrive at Tham Luang.

the coast, gathering intelligence along the border, and stopping terrorist attacks. They also conduct underwater bomb disposal and mine defusing, which explains why they are some of the most highly trained open-water divers in the country. The SEALs are such experienced divers that many of them start a second career as scuba-diving instructors after they retire.

Thai Navy SEAL commander Rear Admiral Apakorn Yuukongkaew

The SEALs' commander, Rear Admiral Apakorn Yuukongkaew, accompanies his unit to Tham Luang. He is respected by his troops for being an even-tempered leader who rarely shouts. He has a reputation for keeping his word and for calm persistence in the face of adversity — which is exactly what this mission will require. Rear Admiral Apakorn agrees that there is no reason to fear the worst about the Wild Boars. "I believe they're all still alive, but they might be exhausted," he tells reporters. "We should get good news today."

Seeing the SEALs, strong and fit, in their dive gear and wet suits, gives the families hope. They look like superheroes, here to save the day. Surely these men will be able to find their children. But what no one outside Tham Luang understands is just how treacherous the water conditions inside the cave actually are.

Thai Navy SEALs wade through the fierce current inside Tham Luang.

7.

The Dangers of Cave Diving

June 25, 2018

JUST BEFORE DAWN on June 25, the SEAL divers enter the flooded Sam Yaek junction. Their headlamps cast an eerie green glimmer in the murky water. They each carry a single steel cylinder on their back that has been pumped full of compressed (or squeezed) air. Like soda pop in a bottle, the air inside the tanks is stored at high pressure. In order to make use of it, the divers have to breathe through a regulator, which lowers the pressure of the air as they inhale.

The SEALs also carry multiple regulators for backup, and they each wear a buoyancy vest that connects to their air supply. By adding or releasing air from their vest, the SEALs can control how much they float or sink in the water. They each wear a face mask with headlamps to light the way, and a wet suit to prevent the cold water from wicking away their body heat.

The SEALs manage to find the left-hand opening that Vern Unsworth has described to them. The opening is much smaller than they had anticipated and is covered by about six feet (two meters) of water.

One SEAL sticks his foot inside the hole. There is space beyond, but the passage has been clogged with rocks and mud. Using a steel pipe, the SEALs hack at the opening, pushing away the debris and widening it. Even then, it's too small for them to fit through with their back-mounted air cylinders. In a highly risky move, they shrug off their tanks and push the metal cylinders ahead of them down the passage. It's hard going through the current, which rushes around the SEALs with the force of a river and threatens to slam them against the passage walls. If you've ever played with a garden hose and covered up the nozzle with your thumb, then you know that when flowing water is forced through a smaller hole,

Vern Unsworth and Thai rescue workers at Sam Yaek junction

ALL THIRTEEN

it speeds up. This is what the SEALs experience as they try to fight their way through the narrow, jagged passages beyond Sam Yaek.

Though the Navy SEALs have spent hundreds of hours diving in the open water, none of them have dived in caves. They certainly have never encountered a cave as hostile to diving as Tham Luang.

Underwater caverns can be some of the most spectacular environments on earth, filled with crystal-clear water in every shade of blue and green, dripping with Candy Land–like stalactites. But no matter how clear the water or beautiful the scenery, diving in a cave is dangerous business. Unlike diving in the open sea, where you can easily return to the air above, cave diving takes you far from the surface, down dark and twisting passages. That is where the danger lies.

Your body has evolved so well for a life spent in air that you may take it for granted. The lenses of your eyeballs are adapted to see objects through air. Your skeleton effortlessly holds up your body against the weight of 50 miles (80 kilometers) of air in the atmosphere pressing down on you. With no conscious effort on your part, your diaphragm, a muscle beneath your stomach, expands and contracts, which causes your lungs to fill with this precious gas.

But the moment you enter the water, all of that changes.

Even the world's greatest free divers (people who dive without an oxygen tank) can hold their breath for only about ten minutes before they have to swim back to the surface. When you hold your breath, your body gradually uses up the oxygen that your cells need to function, and it starts producing carbon dioxide. The carbon dioxide builds up, sending a signal to your diaphragm and the other muscles around your rib cage to inflate your lungs. If you keep holding your breath, your diaphragm will spasm painfully. Your body wants to breathe. Your lungs want to expand. Your mouth wants to open and gasp. And if you are still underwater when this happens, you will drown.

Cave diving's ultimate danger, of course, is running out of air before you can return to the surface. But there are a hundred ways to get yourself into that grim situation. Your equipment could malfunction, and you could be too far from the cave exit to get out in time. You could get physically trapped in a tight squeeze, or your gear could snag on a rock or on the cave wall.

Visibility (how far you can see) is crucial for making your way through a cave and for finding your way out. A dropped flashlight or dead batteries will plunge you into complete and total darkness, leaving you groping along the cave walls. Without light from the surface to orient you, down becomes up, and you can think you are swimming for the exit when you are actually pushing farther inside the cave.

Dropped lights aren't the only way to get lost. Many cave passages have a layer of fine silt on the bottom that has filtered out of the water over long periods of time. One wrong flick of your fins, and you could stir up a silt cloud that instantly turns the clear water into a murky mess. You could get lost in a cave's labyrinth-like tunnels and spend all your precious air reserves searching for the way out.

The Thai SEALs don't seem to know the number one rule in cave diving: always use a single, continuous guideline. The first group of divers to enter a cave attach a guideline to the walls and boulders as they go, setting a path that others can follow, while always maintaining a link to the exit. Until that vital line is laid, the first group of divers must make their way slowly and carefully. The same stalactites and stalagmites that cause tourists to ooh and aah in a dry cave become real hazards to a cave diver. The jutting formations can tangle a line, or if they are sharp enough, they can slice it clean through. In water as murky as in Tham Luang, divers would have no idea they were approaching a rock formation until their head banged straight into it.

The cave's passages are also not straight-line shots from point A to point B. Tham Luang has plenty of false passageways that jut off from the main system and lead nowhere. Divers can easily make a mistake and follow one of these branches, then smack headfirst into a dead end. They must then either turn around and swim back out, or — if the passage is

Stalactites in Tham Luang

too tight to turn in—slowly back up, inch by inch, until they return to where they started.

Incredibly, despite the lack of a guideline, the SEALs manage to get past Sam Yaek and reach an area of higher, dry ground. Here, they see footprints but no other sign of the boys. Beyond them, they see nothing but a passage flooded with dark water. They can go no farther, or they won't have enough air to make the return trip.

When they get back to the junction, they share the bad news with the other SEALs. Even worse, they realize that the water at Sam Yaek is rising higher and higher. And outside the cave, the rain is coming down hard.

Rules to Dive By

Only by following a strict set of rules have divers been able to safely explore caves. These rules were developed by a young cave diver named Sheck Exley in the 1970s. In Florida at that time, cave diving was becoming more popular — and more deadly. So many people had died while cave diving that government officials considered banning it altogether.

Exley was disturbed by the number of cave-diving deaths. He pored over the accident reports for these dives and discovered that many who died were experienced open-water divers who had been unprepared for diving in caves. In fact, it's possible that their comfort in the open ocean had given them a false sense of confidence, which led to their deaths.

Exley developed a set of rules that saved lives and that are still followed by cave divers today:

1. Always use a single, continuous guideline from the entrance of the cave throughout the dive.
2. Always use the "Thirds Rule": Use one-third of your air supply on the way in, use one-third on the way out, and save one-third in case you run into an emergency.
3. Avoid deep diving in caves.
4. Avoid panic by building up experience slowly and being prepared for emergencies.
5. Carry at least three lights per diver.
6. Use the safest possible scuba equipment.
7. Avoid stirring up silt on the bottom.
8. Practice emergency procedures with your partner before diving, and review them often.
9. Always carry equipment for emergencies and know how to use it.
10. Never let overconfidence allow you to think it's OK to break any of these rules.

A cave diver follows a guideline.

Cave biologist Jean Krejca shines her light into a cave's flooded passages.

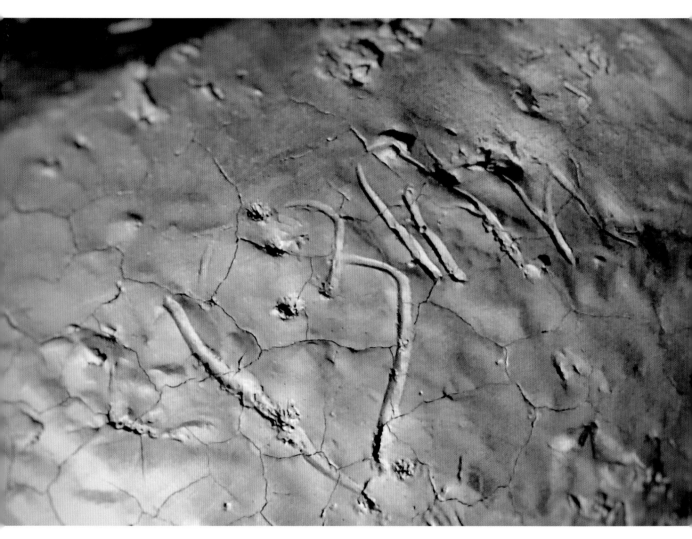

A message written by the Wild Boars as they hoped for rescue

8.

Empty Bellies, Clear Minds

June 26, 2018

THE WILD BOARS are entering their third full day underground. They've spent the first two days trapped in the cave alternating between crying and comforting one another and crying again. Why hasn't anyone found them yet? How long will they have to be there?

Even now that their tears have dried, it's so frustrating to have to sit in one place hour after hour with nothing to do but wait. The Wild Boars are not the sitting type. They want to do something, *anything*.

They keep checking the water that blocks their way out, but it hasn't gone down. They scratch messages into the cave's walls: 26TH OF JUNE: 13 BOYS NEED RESCUING. They have no idea who will see these messages, but at least it gives them something to do.

Bew and Dom tell the others that they once heard of a way out through the back of the cave. But it's *really* far back. Local people tell stories of a man who went deep into Tham Luang and found a shaft lit by moonlight that led to the surface. He climbed up and found himself in an isolated village nestled in the mountain valley. Having lost the hole

Sunlight shines onto a Buddhist altar inside a karst cave.

back to the cave, he stayed in the village for forty years until the day he discovered the cave again and returned back through Tham Luang to his own people.

It's lovely to imagine a beam of pale moonlight shining down from the surface into the cave. It's even better imagining climbing out. But does such a shaft really exist, or is it just a story? The boys have no idea how far underground they are, but it must be hundreds of yards. Even if they could find a shaft that led to the surface, how could they climb up? And what if they go looking for it and get trapped even farther back in the cave?

At least here they have a good supply of fresh water. The water tastes clean, and it hasn't made anyone sick so far. Coach Ek is reluctant to leave such an important resource. In the end, they decide to wait where they are.

By the third day, the boys' tears may have stopped, but their hunger has multiplied. Titan, the youngest, has pains in his stomach from the hunger. He tries not to think about food, but it's so hard not to. He craves the good foods his family makes, like fried rice and northern-style curry paste. He isn't alone. Everyone dreams of food.

Coach Ek urges the boys to rest and to conserve as much energy as possible. When your body is deprived of food, it will lower its metabolism to survive. Metabolism is the rate at which your body converts food into energy. The lower your metabolism, the longer you can survive without eating.

Some mammals can survive for months without food by hibernating. During hibernation, they go into a deep sleep, their metabolism slows, and their body temperature drops, until they wake up in the spring thin and hungry. If only the Wild Boars could hibernate! But humans must keep their body temperature at about 98.6 degrees Fahrenheit (37 degrees Celsius). Even when the boys are resting, their bodies are burning calories just to keep themselves warm. Since they can't get those calories from eating food, they have started to burn through the little fat they had stored up. If a person goes long enough without eating, their body will eventually begin consuming itself to stay warm and stay alive.

It doesn't help that the cave is damp and chilly. It's about 72°F (22°C), which is on the cold side for Thai children, who are used to warmer weather this time of year. The team got soaked when they had to cross the pools of water, and they still haven't managed to dry out completely. The boys tug their shorts over their knees and slip their arms inside their sleeves. They scoop out a ditch in the sand, where they can huddle close and trap the heat radiating off their bodies.

Coach Ek keeps careful track of the flashlights, saving the most powerful ones and flicking only one on at a time whenever they need to get a drink of water. With the lights off, it's pitch-black.

Meditation

Meditating doesn't have to be done in a temple or seated on a mat with your eyes closed. It's something that anyone can practice anytime. It can start with focusing on something simple, like paying close attention to the way your chest rises and falls with every breath. Or it might involve imagining your mind as a room with two windows. When thoughts of hunger, pain, or shame come in through one window, you can notice them, and then let them float right out the other window, keeping the room of your mind clear from all that clutter. When the mind is uncluttered, it allows you to calm your body and see the world more clearly. After all, it was through meditation that the Buddha arrived at the pillars of his great teachings that guide all Buddhists today.

The Buddha taught people how to free themselves from the suffering that is a natural part of life. Trapped in the cave, the boys are indeed suffering—from hunger and fear. Obsessing over their hunger pains, or fantasizing about eating, or succumbing to the worry they may never get out will only make their suffering worse. By meditating

Go into the darkest corner of the darkest room of your house. Shut the door and turn off the light. After a few minutes, when your eyes adjust, it's likely that some photons of light will somehow find their way to your eyeballs. Not so inside a cave.

The total darkness of caves can cause some people to hallucinate, seeing flares of color at the edges of their vision. Dwell on the darkness too long, and it takes on a heaviness that presses in on you, weighing you down. Professional cavers who spend weeks at a time inside a cave describe a condition they call the Rapture, which is a panic attack that seizes people deep underground. Of all the dangers one can encounter in a cave, losing your mind is the most frightening of all.

Novice monk meditating

and focusing on their breathing, the team can be aware of their physical and emotional pains without dwelling on them.

Meditation can't erase the boys' hunger and doubts, but it can help release its power over them.

Coach Ek is determined not to let his team fall prey to panic. He knows that they will take their cues from him. If he stays cool, they'll be cool. To help them even more, he tells them to meditate.

All the Wild Boars are familiar with the practice of meditation. Like most of the boys, Coach Ek is Buddhist, and he usually leads the team through meditation exercises before a soccer game to get them focused on the match ahead. Just like on the soccer field, the boys follow their coach's guidance. Breath by breath, they each become the master of the one thing they can control inside Tham Luang: their own mind.

Water flowing through Tham Luang

9.

At War with the Water

June 25–26, 2018

IT RAINS HEAVILY ALL DAY on Monday, June 25. Even more water is now pouring into the bowl of Sam Yaek junction from the Monk's Series passage. The current is strong enough to pick up a sandbag and carry it downstream. Even though they are almost certain that the boys didn't go into Monk's Series, Thai authorities place a sentry at the opening to watch for any sign of the team — clothes, shoes, or water bottles — that might flow out with the current.

The water at Sam Yaek rises higher and higher.

Days later, the rescue team will label the main sections of Tham Luang with numbers. The rooms that will eventually be called Chambers 1, 2, and 3 now buzz with the sounds of people and equipment. Royal Thai Army personnel and rescue workers have carried in floodlights to illuminate the dark chambers. They have set up a communications station in Chamber 3: a fifty-year-old field telephone from the Vietnam War era. It's boxy and ugly, but extremely reliable, and at least they don't have to depend on a person hiking messages in and out.

Vern Unsworth, Woranan "Tik" Ratrawiphakkun, and rescue worker Nikornchai Phopluechai discuss a map of the cave system.

Pumps have been installed to try to lower the water levels at Sam Yaek. In the beginning, the pumps run off gasoline. But the fumes from the machines quickly fill the chambers, making working conditions dangerous. Some workers even pass out from the lack of oxygen. The pumps are replaced with electrical versions, but these new machines still require power. Thick electrical cables snake through the passages, connecting all the equipment inside to generators at the surface.

Despite the pumps operating at full capacity, the water inside the cave is still rising. From the rate at which it is rising, Vern knows that water is not only entering Sam Yaek from Monk's Series in the north, but must also be flowing through the main cave passage from the south. Vern doesn't know exactly where the water from the south comes from, but he can tell that it's cold, which means it must be coming from deep underground. It's possible that the water's source begins all the way across the border in Myanmar. With water coming into Tham Luang from both ends, the chance of the levels going down anytime soon is low.

The Thai Navy SEALs again attempt to dive past Sam Yaek, but they get no farther than before. The current is now so strong that if a diver doesn't keep his face head-on to the flow, the water will rip his mask off. On June 26, the water rises so high that it pushes the SEALs and all the other rescue workers out of the Sam Yaek area completely.

Vern emerges from the cave, muddy and discouraged. He tells his partner, Tik, that he's worried the operation is going to end very badly. The SEALs have no shortage of determination and physical strength, but the fact remains that they don't have the equipment or experience to dive in caves.

That afternoon, he lays out the horrendous conditions to the mission commander, Governor Narongsak: the water is cold, the current is strong, and the visibility is so low that it's like trying to dive through a vat of coffee. There are only a handful of people in the world who can dive in water like this, and they must bring those people to Tham Luang immediately.

Vern tells the governor: "Sir, you have one last chance at this rescue, or the boys will die."

US Air Force Major Charles Hodges shakes hands with Thai Army General Bancha Duriyaphan.

10.
The Problem Solvers

June 27–28, 2018

US AIR FORCE MAJOR CHARLES HODGES has been commander of the 320th Special Tactics Squadron stationed in Okinawa, Japan, for just over a week when he gets the call telling him that his team's assistance has been requested by the Thai government. He has followed the situation in northern Thailand on television but doesn't know much beyond the fact that a group of young boys is trapped inside a flooded cave with their coach. His squadron quickly assembles and boards a C-130 transport plane headed for Chiang Rai on the evening of June 27.

Major Hodges is new to commanding a squadron, but his years of training have taught him that good leaders do the following:

- Gather as much information as possible in the beginning.

- Assemble a strong team of people with the right expertise.

- Listen to many different ideas about solving the problem.

- Step back and let their team do what they do best.

Plenty of leaders end up shutting down good solutions because they just can't give up control. Luckily, Major Hodges is not a "My way or the highway" type of leader. He is a little bit like Coach Ek in that way. He knows that his team is one of the best-equipped in the entire Indo-Pacific region for this type of extreme search-and-rescue operation. Members of his squadron have pulled survivors out of collapsed buildings after earthquakes. They have recovered bodies from helicopter crashes over the open ocean. They have rescued downed pilots from behind enemy lines. His team has combat experience, emergency medical experience, and years of open-water diving experience.

But rescuing a group made up almost entirely of children is unusual for them, and it will present special challenges. Major Hodges has four children of his own, and many in his squadron are also parents. He tells his unit that as difficult as it may be, he needs them to leave their emotions behind. If they are going to be useful in this rescue, they can't let their emotions cloud their ability to tackle the problem.

When the team arrives at Tham Luang at 1:00 a.m. on June 28, they get an immediate introduction to just how unique — and difficult — this mission will be. Major Hodges is in the middle of getting an orientation to Chamber 1 when an urgent voice calls them back to the mouth of the cave. As the squadron crosses Chamber 1, their boots slosh through ankle-deep water where only moments before the ground had been dry. Behind them, Thai Navy SEALs and rescue workers rush out, hauling as much equipment as they can carry as water surges higher and fills the cave all the way to the entrance chamber.

It's clear to Major Hodges that this is not going to be a simple cave extraction. He gathers his team in one of the small park headquarters buildings to go over the information they have so far. Even though their squadron has plenty of experience carrying out scuba-diving recoveries in the open ocean, they are no more prepared for cave diving than the Thai SEALs are. If the US team is going to assist the SEALs, it won't be with their diving skills but with their problem-solving skills.

The first thing they need to do is to "establish proof of life," or figure out if the boys and Coach Ek are even alive. If they are, they will urgently need food, water, and medical care. Major Hodges's team brainstorms different ways to find them.

The first option is to drill into the side of the mountain. In 2010, when thirty-three miners were trapped in a collapsed mine in Chile, they were rescued by drilling a hole 2,300 feet, or 700 meters, into the earth and pulling them up to the surface. The Wild Boars are nowhere near that deep underground. If the rescue teams could drill even a small four- to six-inch hole into the cave — just 10 to 15 centimeters across — they could lower a camera or a microphone down and figure out if the boys are still alive.

A second option is to suck enough water out of the cave so that rescuers can simply swim — or, better yet, walk — inside instead of having to dive. The Thai military has set up pumps at the entrance to lower the water levels, but with all the recent rain, the pumps can't keep up with the flow. Major Hodges asks himself, *Who is the very best in the world at pumping out huge amounts of fluid from under the ground?* The answer he comes up with: oil companies. He begins reaching out to oil companies in Thailand to see what type of equipment and expertise they can bring.

The third option is to look for alternative entrances into the cave. In a karst system as long as Tham Luang's, surely there are other openings that lead from the surface into the cave. Locals insist that they know of holes hidden in the forest that enter into Tham Luang. But do the entrances exist — or are they just legends? Everyone decides that they have to give this third option a shot.

Their task is daunting. The Nang Non mountain range is covered in thick jungle. The steady rains and plentiful sunlight of this region of Thailand nurtures forests full of life. Straight-trunked trees called dipterocarps soar overhead, draped in vines that make it impossible to tell where one tree ends and the next one begins. When you stand on top of the mountain and look out, you see nothing but green. It makes for beautiful sightseeing; it makes for horrible hiking. Add to that the muddy, slippery ground from all the rainfall, and you have downright treacherous conditions.

Members of Thailand's national parks department and Royal Thai Army personnel are tasked with leading the overland search. They are joined by Charles Hodges's US Air Force team and thousands of volunteers, including search-and-rescue experts from Australia and China, as well as Vern Unsworth and Sangwut's rescue workers, who have been at Tham Luang since the day they discovered the boys' bikes.

Local guides help to lead groups through the dense brush. These guides are highland indigenous peoples, who have made their home in the valleys between Thailand's northern mountains for centuries. Many migrated into Thailand to escape persecution in their ancestral homeland in Myanmar; others trace their origins to Laos or China. They have their own languages and traditions, and their villages are small and quite isolated from one another. They are very familiar with the forests surrounding their villages, and they lead the search parties to holes they know are deep.

The big question is, How deep do they go?

Among the many volunteers who will join the search is a group from Thailand's far southern Trang province who have made the 1,000-mile journey to Chiang Rai, about 1,600 kilometers. They are professional bird's nest collectors who search caves for cliff swallow nests, which are used to make bird's nest soup, a prized delicacy in Thailand and China. They bring ropes and tough, callused palms. They lower themselves down on the ropes — headfirst and without helmets — into the pitch-black shafts. The squeezes are so tight that searchers have to clear out rocks bit by bit with their hands, passing the debris back out to their teammates behind them.

Governor Narongsak sends helicopters and drones into the sky to scan the terrain and take photographs. The searchers find some shafts

Climbers with ropes hike through the jungle in search of alternative entrances into the cave.

that reach as deep as 100 feet (30 meters) into the mountain, but so far, each one is a dead end. They will not give up, though. They continue combing the mountain, even as more rain falls overhead. When the search teams are too far away to make it back before dark, they curl up on the ground and sleep in the forest.

Back at base camp, plastic tarps have been set up for the boys' families, who have spent day and night in front of the cave, praying. They kneel in front of a spread of fancy desserts, fruit, rice, and sweet drinks, all offerings presented to the Sleeping Lady of Nang Non, the spirit of the

The Spirits Around Us

In Thailand, Buddhism and other spiritual beliefs intertwine. In addition to following the Buddha's teachings, many Thai Buddhists also revere a host of other spirits. You often find carvings and statues of nature spirits, such as water serpents called the Phaya Naga, protecting Buddhist temples. Many Thai homes and businesses have spirit houses somewhere on the property, small wooden shrines that are dedicated to the spirits who watch over the area and honor those who lived there previously. People place offerings of food and flowers at the spirit house as a sign of respect for the spirits. In return, they hope that the spirits will show them good favor and not trouble them.

Nature spirits look over everything: the forests, the rivers, the mountains. Whether you are walking in the jungle or down a busy city street, it's common to see colorful ribbons tied around the trunks of large, old trees—another way to honor the spirits that protect the land. Spirits are everywhere; they can be gentle and protective, or moody and vengeful. Either way, spirits should be treated as respectfully as the living.

cave. The families plead with her to protect their boys. If she is angry, will she please forgive them and let them go? People play gongs and beat drums. They hold up fishing nets in a ritual that symbolizes fishing out the lost boys from the cave.

The families are joined by members of the Wild Boars who didn't go on the adventure with their friends. The boys have all been playing soccer together for years, and everyone feels the loss of the missing twelve. The players who remain are torn between feeling grateful for being safe and feeling guilty for not having gone with the others into Tham Luang. It could

Spirit houses in Mae Sai with offerings placed on them

be them trapped inside. How can they go to sleep at night in the safety of their beds when their friends are trapped underground? As much as soccer is a part of their lives, no one can stomach getting on the field without the other guys.

The boys' teachers and classmates visit the cave, too. They all say the same things. Class is too quiet. It's too hard to study or even pay attention knowing that there is an empty chair where your friend used to sit. Life seems to be on hold, waiting for the twelve boys to come out, for everything to go back to normal.

Kruba Boonchum arrives at Tham Luang.

But then base camp receives a visitor whose presence brings a much-needed ray of hope for the boys' loved ones: the honorable monk Kruba Boonchum. Despite the deep mud, he walks barefoot, as he always does. He is a famous and highly revered forest meditation monk, called by some "the monk of the three nations" because he walks between Thailand, Myanmar, and Laos, praying and teaching his followers. At Tham Luang he is surrounded by people who greet him with deep and respectful bows. He prays with the families and speaks to the spirits surrounding the cave. He listens to what they have to say. Before he leaves,

he tells the Wild Boars' parents not to worry; their sons are just fine, and they will come out in a few days. His calmness puts the families at ease. If Kruba Boonchum says to have hope, how can they do otherwise?

Major Hodges gives the families space. In part, this is because journalists have begun to arrive at Tham Luang in droves. Reporters follow Hodges's team everywhere, and he doesn't want to bring any unwanted attention to the boys' parents. But another reason for keeping his distance is to take his own advice and not get emotionally attached to anyone in the rescue.

His commanding officer calls and asks for an honest assessment. "Do you think you are going to find the kids?"

Major Hodges doesn't sugarcoat things. "No, sir, I don't," he says. "I think of myself as a glass-half-full kind of guy, but I don't see how these kids could still be in there. Caves are not hospitable environments. If they are in there, they're probably dead, and if we're lucky, we will find their remains."

The Thai air force has just deployed an underwater drone to try to push through the freshly flooded entrance passages. It may be able to provide valuable information about what the underwater conditions are like. But even if the drone can get through the water, it won't be able to cross the dry sections of the cave to continue searching for the boys. So far, no one has invented an amphibious robot that can swim through water and then climb onto dry land and keep going. The only way to get into the dark belly of Tham Luang is to send a human being.

Sending in divers is the fourth option Major Hodges's team comes up with, but at the moment, it seems the most impossible. Only the world's very best cave divers would be able to even attempt it.

Major Hodges doesn't know it yet, but that is exactly who has just arrived at Tham Luang.

Tham Luang entrance chamber

11.

The Sump Divers

June 27–28, 2018

WHEN VERN UNSWORTH WARNED Governor Narongsak on June 26 that he had "one last chance" to save the boys, he was initially ignored.

Vern wasn't exactly surprised. In his urgency to help, his emotions had run away from him, and he had raised his voice to the governor when other people were around to hear. Vern had lived in Thailand long enough to understand that he had offended the mission commander.

Luckily, that night, he gets another opportunity to make his case. In a meeting with Thailand's minister of tourism, Vern explains the need for expert cave divers. He scrawls a note for the minister:

Time is running out!

1. *ROB HARPER*
2. *RICK STANTON MBE*
3. *JOHN VOLANTHEN*

They are the world's best cave divers. Please contact them through UK EMBASSY ASAP.

The minister makes the call, but Vern can tell he is skeptical that their problems can be solved by a trio of British amateurs. After all, Thailand's most elite military is on the scene at Tham Luang, plus the US Air Force, plus search-and-rescue experts from Vietnam, China, and Australia. If anyone can locate the missing children, surely it's the team they already have.

And the three men on Vern's list are indeed a trio of amateurs. They have no military ranking. There is no professional organization that pays them for their expertise. Some people might even call what they do a hobby. But that "hobby" just happens to be exactly what is needed to find the boys.

The conditions at Tham Luang are too much for open-water divers to handle. They are too much for even most cave divers to handle. What they need in this situation are divers who can tackle a gnarly, nasty *sump*.

If you want to visualize what a sump is, go into your kitchen, open the cabinet under the sink, and take a look at the pipes. The drainpipe from the sink leads down, then curls upward again before disappearing into the kitchen wall. That low U-shaped section is the sump. When you turn on the faucet, the entire pipe fills with water as it flows out to the sewer. But even when you turn the faucet off, some water will remain trapped in that sump.

This is also what happens inside a cave. Sumps form in cave systems when water erodes the rock unevenly, or when tunnels move around with the shifting and rising of the earth's crust. When a cave floods, water fills its passages. But even after the flood subsides, some water is left behind in the sunken sumps. Some sumps exist year-round. Others fill only after a flood and then gradually drain away.

For cavers, a sump is a major bummer. Until just a few decades ago, these pools of water would be labeled on cavers' maps as "terminal sumps," meaning that was the end of the trail. But cavers know that when you find water in a cave, that water has to go somewhere.

Once cavers started strapping tanks of air on their backs, they could dive through the sumps and explore the caverns beyond. Many cave divers begin as cavers first. They learn diving techniques as a way of getting past the inevitable sump that pops up on their explorations. They then get hooked on the diving, finding that it provides plenty of opportunity for discovery and record setting.

For all of its high moments, diving in sumps is grueling, dangerous work. When you are in the belly of the earth, far from medical help, without any communication with the outside, one slipup can be deadly.

Many of the world's most notorious sumps can be found on the British Isles. Unlike the spacious, crystal-clear water in the caves of Florida or Mexico, British sumps are generally cold, cramped, and murky. It's no wonder that some of the world's best sump divers are members of the British Cave Rescue Council (BCRC). The BCRC is a group of volunteers who specialize in finding and rescuing people (and farm animals!) who are lost or trapped in caves. Every year, the BCRC conducts dozens of rescues all over the UK, and they also coordinate international requests for rescue help. They had been following the situation in Thailand online, so they weren't surprised when they were contacted by the Thai authorities.

As soon as they get the notice from the BCRC, Rick Stanton and his long-time diving partner, John Volanthen, zip to Heathrow Airport, in London, with their colleague Rob Harper, who will support the pair aboveground. While not a diver himself, Rob has fifty years of caving experience and had just been at Tham Luang a few months prior, mapping new passages with his good friend Vern Unsworth.

Rick and John have been called the A-Team. Among cave divers, they are as close to being celebrities as you get. They hold a good share of the world's cave-diving records, but they aren't in it for fame or recognition. It's the satisfaction of figuring out how different parts of a cave system connect and the thrill of stepping into a place where no one else has set foot (or flipped a fin) that push them forward.

Rick, John, and Rob arrive at Chiang Rai airport on the evening of

Rob Harper (in red), John Volanthen (in blue), and Rick Stanton (in black) arrive at Tham Luang.

June 27, and Tik whisks them straight to the cave. Journalists surround them, hounding them for a statement. John Volanthen simply answers, "We've got a job to do."

They hope to get a good look at the cave and start talking through their dive plan. But when Vern leads them inside late that night, Tham Luang shows them right away what a hostile cave she is. In the same event that startles Major Charles Hodges and the US Air Force, the cave floods, sending everyone in a mad scramble for the exit.

If the British divers had any questions about whether this would be an easy cave rescue, Tham Luang has just provided an answer.

The next day, Thursday, June 28, John and Rick "kit up" in their wet suits and gear and enter the flooded Chamber 1. Yesterday they could have walked the entire distance to Chamber 3. Today, thanks to the flash flood, they now have three short sumps to cross before they can even get that far. Electrical cables and wires snake through the water around them. They have gotten repeated assurances from the Thai authorities that all of the power has been shut off, but they are still nervous about being electrocuted.

The water is a cloudy, milky brown. In a cave like Tham Luang, which dries out part of the year, the first floodwaters churn up all the silt and mud that has packed down during the dry season. Not only that, but the water is swirling, moving so quickly that it's eddying in small whirl-pools. The water levels are continuing to rise. Normally, if Rick and John had found these conditions, they would have turned right back around. But given the urgency of finding the boys, they decide to see if they can push past Chamber 3 and figure out what lies beyond.

They slosh through half-flooded Chamber 2, then dive through two short sumps. When they pass the third sump and surface in Chamber 3, they hear voices.

Rescue teams congregate in the entrance chamber to Tham Luang.

THE SUMP DIVERS

Have they found the boys? No way. Surely that was too easy.

As they shine their lights into the dark cave, they realize they haven't found children. They have found four adult men!

The men are employees of the Thai Well Water Association who have spent the last several days working on the water-pumping operation in Chamber 3. At first, Chamber 3 was dry, and it was well stocked with food and drinking water so workers didn't have to make the strenuous hike back to the entrance so often. Like everyone in Chamber 3, the Well Water Association employees worked long, grueling hours, and they had collapsed in a dark corner of the chamber to catch a few hours of sleep.

While they were resting, the floodwaters began rising quickly. The Thai Navy SEALs evacuated the chamber, but in the rush to get everyone out, they overlooked the sleeping workers. The checkpoint at the cave entrance wasn't well organized at that time, and any record of the four men being inside the cave was lost. Because of all the people working

Rescue workers stand in waist-deep water in Chamber 1.

inside the cave, oxygen levels were slightly lower than outside. This can make people feel groggy and have trouble thinking clearly, which may explain why the men didn't wake during the clamor to evacuate. When they finally did rouse from sleep, they found themselves alone in the half-flooded cave.

By the time Rick and John find them, the men are cold and terrified. The workers had tried to swim out but couldn't make it through the first sump. They have spent the last twenty-four hours standing in waist-deep water, praying that someone would find them.

Rick and John aren't prepared for a rescue. They haven't brought extra tanks or face masks. None of the workers have ever scuba-dived before. The water in Chamber 3 is littered with abandoned equipment, and the surface swirls with the sheen of gasoline. The conditions are awful. But the water is rising by the minute, which means they need to act fast.

The divers decide to do a "snatch," or unplanned, rescue, which will require them to take turns crossing the sumps with the stranded men. Rick takes off his gear and gives it to one of the workers, who is guided through the first sump by John. John then swims the gear back through to the waiting workers. They continue this process, taking turns, until the entire group is through.

The relieved and grateful workers emerge into the open, feeling lucky to be alive. Rick and John are lucky, too. If the water had come up quickly, the diver who had taken off his gear would have been trapped on the far side of the sump with no air supply.

The experience has been sobering for both Rick and John. They now know how appalling the water conditions in Tham Luang really are. The men they rescued were jittery, and they barely got out without panicking. If the boys ultimately have to be extracted from the cave using the same method, they'll have to dive even deeper and swim even farther.

But in order to do that, the rescue team will have to find them first.

Coach Ek on the soccer field

12.
Coach Ek

June 28, 2018

THE WILD BOARS are resting in Chamber 9 when they hear a sudden, gurgling *swoosh*. Coach Ek quickly flicks on the flashlight and shines it into the darkness. Water is rushing up toward them. Behind them is a very steep slope of rock and gravel that rises about 30 feet (nine meters) into a formation called an aven, a high vertical chamber that doesn't reach the surface. The boys clamber up this slope as quickly as they can. In less than an hour, the water surges almost nine feet, or three meters.

How far will the flood rise? Will it continue edging closer? Thankfully, it stops before it reaches the boys. But now they are trapped at the top of this gravelly hill, on a relatively flat space the size of a small bedroom. The hill butts up against the cave wall on one side. Below, water curls around them, flowing past like a river. Before, it had seemed as though the water blocking their way had flowed toward them out of Sam Yaek. But now the current is moving in the opposite direction, gushing from somewhere out of the depths of Tham Luang.

What they don't realize is that the water that trapped them to begin with had flowed in from Monk's Series. But now, with all the rain that has been pummeling the mountain outside, the cave has begun to flood from the main passage as well. The Wild Boars are doubly trapped.

Even in their perilous state, the boys hold on to hope. They make plans for what they will do after they are rescued. They make a solemn promise: When they get out of the cave, they will look after one another forever. They will never go anywhere without telling the others where they are.

One thing that keeps the boys from sinking into despair is thinking about their families. The faces of their mothers, fathers, grandparents, siblings, and friends fill their minds, both in dreams and wakefulness. It brings them comfort to imagine future moments with the people they love.

Coach Ek has few loved ones left alive to dream of. Most of the people he loves are here in the cave with him. Ek was born across the border in the hills of Myanmar, in the Shan region. When he was only nine years old, he lost both parents and his brother in one sudden rush of illness, leaving him in the care of his grandmother.

Migrant children face tough odds in Thailand: it's estimated that half do not enroll in school and only one-quarter are accessing medical care. When migrant children lose their parents, their struggles only increase. Unless another family member is able to care for them, children can end up homeless and living on the streets, where they are vulnerable to being kidnapped, abused, or becoming addicted to drugs.

Luckily, Ek did not end up on the streets. At the age of nine, his grandmother sent him to a temple in Lamphun, a town south of Mae Sai, where he went through the ceremony to become a nain, or a novice monk. This is a common experience for Thai boys, but Ek lived as a nain for a much longer time than most — almost eleven years.

Being a young monk is not without its challenges. Monks rise before the sun, at around 4:00 a.m. They take their morning walk to meet with

A novice monk accepts a meal prepared by a local family.

villagers and receive food from them. Back at the temple, they eat and pray. They may eat another small, light meal at noon, but after that they practice spiritual fasting and eat nothing until sunrise the next day. The purpose of fasting in the evening is to practice discipline and allow the monks to focus on their studies and meditation.

That's the idea, anyway. But for a new monk in training, life at the temple is hard to get used to. Sitting in meditation is uncomfortable. Your back aches. Your empty belly rumbles. Your mind churns with thoughts of food or your bed back at home. How are you supposed to keep doing this? It seems impossible!

But then you make it through that first day, and then another day, and then a week. You realize that both your body and your mind are stronger than you thought.

Once you have conquered one challenge, you begin to wonder: What else have you told yourself is impossible? What else is there that you believed you could not overcome? Maybe the idea of impossible is only in your mind.

Thailand's Stateless People

Coach Ek and three other members of the Wild Boars team are "stateless," meaning they do not have official Thai citizenship and legally belong to no country. It is difficult to get an accurate count of the number of stateless people living in the shadows in Thailand, but it could be as many as 3.5 million—many of them children.

For centuries, Southeast Asia has been a place of migrations, both large and small. Many of those who cross the border into Thailand from Myanmar, Laos, and China come seeking work and better opportunities. For some, their futures are so bleak in their home countries that staying to work in Thailand without official permission is worth the risk of being arrested or deported. Others cross into Thailand daily, working on one side of the border and sleeping on the other.

Violence and persecution also drive migrants into Thailand. In the Shan region of Myanmar, where Coach Ek was born, armed conflict has pushed civilians across the border seeking safety. Other groups, such as the Rohingya of Myanmar, have fled their ancestral land because they are persecuted and murdered by their own government. These refugees have nowhere else to go, and their fate depends on whether neighboring countries will show compassion toward them. As of 2018, Thailand refused to recognize the Rohingya as refugees and either imprisoned them or sent them back to Myanmar, where they face continued violence and even death.

Stateless people in Thailand are supposed to be allowed to go to school and get medical care. But without government documents, they can't attend college, apply for higher-paying jobs, vote, buy land, or travel outside of the country. Even children born on Thai soil can end up stateless if their parents do not fill out the proper paperwork to get them a birth certificate. Sometimes parents are too afraid to register their Thai-born children because they are stateless themselves, and they fear the authorities. In this way, the cycle of statelessness continues.

Mountains at the border of Myanmar and Thailand

Thailand has pledged to reduce the number of stateless people by clearing the barriers to their citizenship. But racism, discrimination, and a lack of political will have slowed the reform process. In the meantime, stateless children in Thailand continue to be among the most vulnerable to poverty, disease, and human trafficking.

Some people, such as Wild Boar team member Adul, manage to thrive despite the many obstacles stacked against them. Faced with violence and few prospects for the future, Adul's parents secretly smuggled him from Myanmar across the border into Mae Sai when he was only six years old. He has been in the care of his church ever since and goes to a nearby school. Adul's principal has called him the "best of the best" and says that "stateless children have a fighting spirit that makes them want to excel."

Coach Ek certainly possesses that same fighting spirit. Without it, he would never have survived the hardships his own country has burdened him with.

Wat Doi Wao, in Mae Sai

When he was twenty years old, Ek left Lamphun and moved to Mae Sai. He spent almost all his time volunteering at Wat Doi Wao, a serene temple perched high on a hill overlooking the border into Myanmar. He impressed the senior monk there, who noticed that the quiet young man seemed to work particularly well with children. He was patient and kind with them and loved to play games. Children trusted him and listened to him when they wouldn't listen to anyone else.

Even though Ek wasn't a monk anymore, he preferred to stay at the temple. He never got into trouble. He didn't go out late, drink alcohol, smoke, or bother anyone. Even when he would take trips outside of Mae Sai, it was almost always to visit temples in neighboring towns. For Ek, a temple was a safe place. It was home.

Though Ek always struck people as friendly and cheerful, he also possessed the gentle wisdom of someone who has suffered deeply. He seemed destined to become a full monk one day, and everyone knew he would be a great one.

Aside from his Buddhist faith, there was one thing that Coach Ek held above all others: soccer. Ek's father had loved the beautiful game with his whole heart, and he passed that passion down to his son. In those lonely, aching days after Ek lost his family to illness, he comforted himself by dreaming that someday he would lead a soccer team of his own. When

Altar inside Wat Doi Wao

Buddhism in Thailand

About 488 million people call themselves Buddhists today, and most live in Asia. Buddhists follow the teachings of a man named Siddhartha Gautama, who was born more than 2,500 years ago in India. He became the Buddha when he reached enlightenment, or a deep understanding of life and the universe. He passed that understanding on through his teachings, which show people how to live good lives. While all Buddhists follow the Buddha's teachings, each country and culture practices the religion in its own way. For most Thai Buddhists, temples, and the monks who live in them, are at the center of religious and everyday life.

People visit their local temple to "make merit," a term that includes making offerings, giving donations, and doing good work. People go to the temple for religious ceremonies, festivals, funerals, or just to stop by and visit with the monks when they need advice or prayer. Until about a hundred years ago, when Thailand developed public schools, temples were also the primary places for children to get an education.

It is very common for boys and men in Thailand to spend time as a nain, or a novice monk. Some Thais believe that a boy cannot reach

the head coach of the Wild Boars hired him as an assistant, it was like a dream coming true.

In the years that Ek has been with the team, he has gradually strengthened the players on and off the field by teaching them what he learned as a monk. And now that they are trapped in the cave, his pregame meditations have turned out to be vital training — not just for the boys, but for Coach Ek himself. He has led his "little brothers" through tough moments before. He reminds them how strong they are. After all, this is the group who bikes up mountains and swims in rivers — the group who manhood without serving as a nain for at least a short time. Boys as young as nine years old may go to the temple in the summer for a few weeks or even months at a time. In the nain ceremony, the boy's head is shaved and then washed with a blessing. Long hair was once a sign of status and wealth. Monks shave their head to symbolize that they are leaving their old lives behind. The young novice is given sunset-colored robes to wear. These robes are so long and complicated that just getting dressed in the morning is often the young monk's first challenge!

Thai monks take an oath to not own possessions or handle money. They are not allowed to buy food for themselves or cook their own meals. They depend completely on their community to provide for them. In early morning, the monks walk barefoot into their village. Local people come out to greet them (also barefoot, as a sign of respect) and scoop the food that they have cooked that morning into the monks' bowls.

A village cares for its monks and its temples, and the temples, in turn, care for anyone who needs help.

gets all the way to the end of a cave with no fear. They are stronger than they even realize.

Sadly, Ek knows from his personal experience just how strong children can be. And so, as hard as it is to ask the boys to endure another night in the cave — and then another, and another — he knows they have it in them.

Keep fighting, he tells them. People are looking for us. They will find us.

Keep fighting.

Rain pummels the rescuers at Tham Luang base camp.

13.

The Water Expert

June 28–29, 2018

ON THURSDAY, JUNE 28, a young man named Thanet Natisri arrives at the park entrance to Tham Luang. It's only a tenth of a mile up the road to base camp, but it takes his car more than an hour to get there. Trucks carrying equipment and supplies clog the road. Military personnel, rescue workers, and journalists are packed tightly together in the small parking lot outside the headquarters building. The ditch along the roadside is practically a creek, filled with thousands of gallons of water being pumped out of the cave. This water is Thanet's reason for being here.

Thanet is an American citizen living in Marion, Illinois, who was born in Thailand. Like many immigrants to America, he has worked hard doing a lot of different jobs. He is currently an architecture student, a restaurant owner, and, as of recently, a water expert. He learned about working with groundwater (water that exists in the soil and rock underground) from his father-in-law, who owns an engineering company in Thailand. Thanet and his father-in-law were working on a project near Bangkok to refill depleted water reservoirs when they got the call from the Thai army to help with the water situation at Tham Luang.

When Thanet finally reaches base camp, he checks in with the person who called him to Tham Luang, army colonel Singhanat Losuya. But Colonel Singhanat hardly has time to speak with him. The prime minister, General Prayut Chan-o-cha, is coming, and everyone is scrambling to get things in order for the head of Thailand's government. Busy and flustered, Colonel Singhanat asks Thanet to go help the team investigating drilling into the mountain to find the boys.

When Thanet finds the drilling team, he's shocked to discover that the only maps they have are two-dimensional, which means they don't contain any information about how high the mountain is or what it looks like inside. It can take days to drill through limestone, so the team has to find the thinnest place between the surface and the cave. For that, they'll need highly specialized seismic mapping equipment.

That night and most of the next day, Thanet darts around the camp, asking one official after another to put in the order for the equipment, but he can't get anyone to listen to him.

Thanet feels so frustrated. Without a proper map, finding the boys inside the mountain is like finding a needle in a haystack — a haystack made of solid rock.

But he can't just sit there doing nothing. He has come to the mountain to help, and he's not going to leave just because things have gotten difficult. He has to find a different way. It was water that brought him here in the first place, so Thanet decides to turn his attention to the water.

Millions of gallons of water are gushing out of the pipes at the main entrance of Tham Luang. At this point, every pump the Thais have been able to find is stationed at the opening, sucking up water and dumping it out of the cave mouth. It's not working. The rains have stopped now, but the water inside the cave remains as high as ever. With that much water, the current is ferocious — much too dangerous to dive through.

Thanet knows that they won't make a dent in the water levels by using only the pumps they have now. The cave's catchment area, or the

area that catches the rainfall and drains it into the mountains, is more than 10,000 acres (40.5 square kilometers). The current pumping operation is similar to trying to drain a child's swimming pool with a straw while the hose is on full blast.

Thanet knows that the ground underneath the cave is completely saturated, like a wet sponge. Any more water that flows into the system will have nowhere to go except into the cave passages. If they want to lower the water levels in the cave, they need to suck some of that groundwater out from the bottom. That will make room for the water in the flooded passages to sink into the earth, and it might lower the levels enough to send in divers.

Thanet has searched his maps for any other places where water flows out of the mountain. He sees that there is another cave nearby at a lower elevation called Sai Tong. There, a creek flows out of the cave mouth into a small pond. Colonel Singhanat tells Thanet that local people say the two caves are connected to each other. If that's true, the water in Tham Luang could be drained out through the pond at Sai Tong.

Sai Tong pond before the rescue operation began

Thanet Natisri stands watch as workers excavate holes at Sai Tong pond.

When Thanet arrives at Sai Tong park, he finds the pond in front of the cave entrance. The pond is usually a calm, lovely blue-green color, but today it is gurgling up, filling with brown water. This is great! The water must be coming from Tham Luang—the two caves must be connected.

Thanet wants to drill under the pond, widening the openings where the water is gurgling out so that they can pump more water away from the cave. Now he just needs drills. In a happy stroke of luck, a group of groundwater engineers happened to overhear Thanet's conversations at base camp about pumping out the groundwater. These engineers are also looking for ways to make themselves useful, and they offer up their equipment—fifteen drilling rigs—for Thanet to use at Sai Tong.

It is now 9:00 p.m. Thanet has been working for fifteen hours straight. But there is no rest for the weary. He gives the go-ahead to start drilling.

The next morning, the Thai army assigns four hundred soldiers and members of the Groundwater Well Association of Thailand to assist him. Finally, he has a team of people who can help him get things done. With his team in tow, Thanet begins the drive back to Sai Tong pond. On the way, he sees a vehicle parked on the side of the road that looks like a cross between a rocket ship and a drag racer.

"Slow down, slow down!" he tells his driver.

Thanet hops out of the truck and greets the men standing with the vehicle. They are farmers from central Thailand, and the funky rocket ship on wheels is a homemade super-pump.

Drilling at Sai Tong pond

Colonel Singhanat and Thanet Natisri examine data at Sai Tong.

On the central plains of Thailand, farmers have a lot of problems getting enough water to their crops. During the hot, dry season, they assemble homemade pumps to pull water out of nearby rivers and canals for their fields. Years of innovation (and a little competition among neighboring farms) have resulted in some of the fastest, most efficient pumps in the country. Their souped-up pumps can move 1.6 million gallons of water (more than 6,000 cubic meters) an hour at full capacity. That's a lot of water!

This is Thai ingenuity at its finest. The Thai people have a well-earned reputation for making things with whatever they have at hand.

The homemade super-pumps are nicknamed Phaya Naga, after a magical water beast in Thai mythology.

The farmers explain that they've driven more than 500 miles (800 kilometers) to help out and have been sitting at the roadside for days, hoping to be of use to the rescue. But so far, no one has taken them up on their offer.

Thanet smiles. "If you guys want a job, I have just the job for you."

Super-pumps at work at Sai Tong

Rescue workers wait with heavy machinery at Tham Luang.

14.
The Rescue Stalls

June 30, 2018

THE PARENTS OF THE WILD BOARS do not feel hopeless, but they do feel helpless. They want to do something, *anything*, besides sitting and waiting to hear good news. They pray. They hold each other. They don't give up. But with every day that passes, the waiting becomes harder. The mountain looms over them, tall and solid. Somewhere deep in that mass of rock they know their children are waiting for them. They watch all these military personnel and rescue experts go inside. How is it possible that no one has found them yet?

The parents bring their sons' clothing from home to give to K-9 police units on the mountain. They hope that the police dogs' keen sense of smell can detect what humans have so far been unable to find out: where the boys are located.

But even the dogs come up short. It's becoming clearer and clearer that the boys are so deep inside Tham Luang that detecting their location from the surface is going to be impossible. The only way to find out where they are is for someone to go in and spot them with their own eyes.

From left to right: Major Charles Hodges, Master Sergeant Derek Anderson, Vern Unsworth, Rob Harper (in red), and John Volanthen

John Volanthen and Rick Stanton are the two people with the best chance of being able to do this. The trouble is, ever since the snatch rescue of the workers on June 28, they have refused to reenter Tham Luang.

The swift current and low visibility not only make it hard to swim—they make it impossible to lay a guideline. Without a line, any sump diver who enters those passages is putting his life in danger.

Rick and John aren't just worried about their own lives. If anything goes wrong, and one of them perishes inside Tham Luang, it will make the whole situation more dangerous for everybody.

A dead body requires a recovery. Rick's experience as a firefighter has trained him to be unemotional about such things, but trying to maneuver a lifeless body through the twists and turns of a sump is a grim and dangerous task. When cave divers perish, they often do so in the worst and most treacherous sections of a cave. A drowning diver often flails about in a panic, getting tangled and wrapped in their guideline, which makes extracting their body even trickier.

Another reason Rick and John don't want to continue is that they know they are some of the only people in the world who can pull this mission off. If they die, the operation is sunk. They think it's foolish for anyone to dive, and they speak their minds plainly to the SEAL officers, even when their troops are present. They refuse to dive in Tham Luang on June 29 or 30. The Thai military think the two men are rude, and they can't understand why these supposedly expert divers won't do the one job they were flown in to do. In turn, Rick and John can't understand why the Thais won't listen to them about the risks.

Relationships between the diving team and the Thai authorities become tense. But even though the teams are having trouble understanding each other, everyone shares the same goal: finding the kids and getting them out.

That common mission now unites thousands of men and women gathered at Tham Luang from all over the world. Professional divers from Denmark, Finland, Belgium, and China have come to lend their expertise.

Ben Reymenants, a Belgian diver who has come up from the dive shop he runs on the Thai island of Phuket, is one of the only other divers besides Rick and John with the skills to lay guideline inside of Tham Luang. In the days prior, he battled the ferocious current to help set up a guideline all the way to Sam Yaek. He also agrees that the conditions have become way too dangerous. But when he tells one of the Thai Navy SEAL officers that he will no longer dive in the cave, he doesn't get the reaction he expects.

The officer listens to his description of how terrible the conditions are. He understands the diver's reservations. He thanks Ben for his service thus far, but tells him that the Thai SEALs are prepared to do anything at any cost to find the boys. They can't abandon their mission, even

Stay Cool

In the UK and the US, it's acceptable — even admired — to speak your mind. But in Thai culture, respect and good graces are more important. Correct manners infuse everyday life, even in the simple act of saying hello. When Thais greet each other or when they express gratitude, they wai. When you wai to someone, you press your palms together in front of you and bow slightly. Who wais first, how high you hold your hands, and how deeply you bow all depend on the age and relationship of the people greeting each other. You are always expected to show older and more senior-ranking people more respect.

The British divers likely didn't see a problem with talking to the SEAL officers frankly in front of their troops, but for Thais, doing so causes the commander to "lose face," which is the height of disrespect. Differences in speaking style might also have caused problems. In Western countries, a person might raise their voice when they want to get their point across. In a disagreement, they might raise their voice louder and louder. But for Thais, shouting is not only disrespectful; it also shows that you can't keep cool. There is an expression in Thai — jai yen — which means having a "cool heart." It describes a person who is patient and calm. Someone who can't have a cool heart is viewed as immature and impulsive. When you lose your cool, people lose respect for you. The more you shout, the less likely people are to listen.

though it's deadly dangerous. If diving is the only way to find the boys, then the SEALs are prepared to dive themselves.

Everyone is moved by the Thai SEAL team's determination and bravery. But based on their many years of expertise, the UK divers know that neither determination nor bravery will be what rescues the boys. If they

Belgian diver Ben Reymenants (left, in a Thai Navy SEAL shirt) discusses a map with US Air Force personnel.

are going to be successful, it will be planning, preparation, and sticking to the rules that does it. They explain to the SEAL commander that they will stay on the mountain, but at the very least, they need more and better equipment, starting with stronger line to withstand the force of the current inside the cave. Their request is immediately granted, and soon a truck pulls up with hundreds of yards of strong climbing rope to use as guidelines.

Everyone agrees to wait and see what the next day will bring. Given the appalling conditions thus far, the British divers can't imagine that the water will improve. But they've waited this long—they are willing to wait at least one day more.

US Air Force personnel, Thai military officials, and representatives from a Thai engineering company examine a map.

15.

The Beautiful Game

June 30, 2018

THE WILD BOARS are starving.

They are grateful to be able to fill their bellies with water, but it doesn't stop the gnawing hunger. The water flowing through the cave has become much clearer now, so they simply drink straight from the stream. The only upside of not having any solid food is that now they don't have to deal with solid wastes either. For the first couple of days, the boys had crossed the water that surrounds their gravelly perch to go to a bank of sand on the other side of the chamber to take care of "business." Now they just pee downstream. Even so, the enclosed space makes it impossible to escape the stink of human waste.

The boys have all started to lose what little body fat they had to begin with. If they have to go on much longer without food, their bodies will begin burning muscle. Any longer than that, and their internal organs will begin to shut down. Their bodies will put their last reserves into keeping their hearts, brains, and kidneys going. Once these vital organs start to suffer, death is not far behind.

The boys haven't reached that dire point yet. But they are painfully cold. When you don't have enough food, your body can lose heat faster than it warms itself up. If your temperature dips below 95°F (35°C), you enter hypothermia, a dangerous state that can cause your heart to fail. Being submerged in water — even relatively warm water — will subject you to hypothermia much faster than if you are dry. The Wild Boars are luckily not submerged, but even on their sandy hill, they can't stay completely dry. A cave is a wet place, and the moisture clings to their clothes and skin. They shiver. The only thing that keeps them warm is huddling together.

Thi sets his watch with two alarms to tell the team when it's morning and night. At least they can try to maintain a regular schedule. But even when they're huddled close together, sleep doesn't come easily, and it doesn't last long. It's hard to get comfortable on the gritty ground, and the constant ache of hunger keeps them awake. We all need sleep to survive. Without it, the immune system gets weaker, people have trouble thinking clearly, and hallucinations can occur.

The boys could hardly be in a more desolate place. But even though they have no food, no warmth, and little sleep, they do have the one thing that is invaluable in a crisis: the will to survive.

This is a phrase that pops up repeatedly in true accounts of survival. Whether the situation is a shipwreck, a prisoner of war camp, or being lost in the mountains, having the will to carry on is sometimes the only thing that separates survivors from victims. Despair can kill as surely as starvation or cold.

People who have never faced challenges often fare the worst in a survival situation because they have no experience meeting obstacles and coming out successfully on the other side. But that is exactly what the Wild Boars had been doing during their adventures together. Even though being trapped in a cave is much harder than riding a bike up a mountain or going on a strenuous hike, the boys know how it feels to push their bodies to their limits. And, perhaps most importantly, through

STAGES OF HYPOTHERMIA

STAGE: MILD
Core Body Temperature: 90–95°F (32–35°C)
  BODY'S RESPONSES:

INITIAL RESPONSES:
- Shivering
- Increased blood pressure
- Increased heartbeat
- Rapid breathing
- Blood vessels contract.

OVER TIME:
- Impaired judgment
- Apathy (not caring)
- Lack of coordination
- Slurred speech
- Decrease in blood volume

STAGE: MEDIUM
Core Body Temperature: 82.4–90°F (28–32°C)
  BODY'S RESPONSES:

- Shivering stops.
- Decreased heart rate
- Decreased breathing rate
- Pupils dilate (widen).
- Chambers of the heart operate out of rhythm.
- Loss of reflexes
- Lowered blood pressure
- Loss of consciousness

STAGE: SEVERE
Core Body Temperature: Less than 82.4°F (28°C)
  BODY'S RESPONSES:

- Nonreactive pupils
- Ceasing of breath (apnea)
- Ceasing of urination
- Shortness of breath due to fluid buildup in lungs
- Electrical activity of the heart is irregular or slowed.
- Coma

Schoolchildren play a game of soccer between classes in Pha Mee, a village in the mountains above Tham Luang.

ALL THIRTEEN

their time on the soccer field, they know what it feels like to work as a team to tackle something that seems impossible.

Every soccer player at every level knows what it feels like to be losing. It's not fun. Your team is one or even two goals down, your legs feel like jelly, your lungs are on fire, and there are just minutes left on the clock. At that point, your team has a few options. You can pull everyone back to defense and try not to let any more shots through. The seconds will tick by as slow as molasses, and your best hope is that the score just doesn't get any worse.

You can also give up the game altogether. This happens even in the professional leagues. It's over — why fight it? This is when the game can become a total blowout, when the other team barrels through your sluggish defenders, and you watch shot after shot rocket past your too-slow feet. The ref blows his whistle. The other players cheer. You are numb. The game ended long ago.

The last option is the hardest and perhaps the rarest to see. But when it happens, oh, how the fans roar.

Ignore the clock. Ignore your jelly legs. Ignore the score and the odds of eking out a win. Push up your defensive line. Pull your goalie out of the box. Dig deep, and then deeper, and find some last reserve of energy that you were sure you spent already. Thumb your nose at the odds and leave it all on the field.

Coach Ek knows that he needs to give the boys a sense of purpose, something to keep them from thinking about their odds of survival. "Do we want to sit and wait for someone to find us?" he asks. "Or do we want to try to help ourselves?"

For the boys, there is only one option. They pick up stones and use them to dig at the base of the cave wall. Taking turns, they each dig a little bit with rocks and with their bare hands. One yard, then two, then three.

They might not be on the soccer field, but the Wild Boars are not giving up the game.

Students at Mae Sai Prasitsart school pray for the success of the rescue.

16.
Going Back In

July 1, 2018

THE BOYS HAVE BEEN TRAPPED inside the mountain for one week and one day. Their story has consumed the nation. Round-the-clock news footage of Nang Non gives what few updates are available, showing clip after clip of rain clouds, flooded riverbanks, and streams of water. The entire country is glued to televisions and mobile phones, watching the coverage.

Schools hold special assemblies to gather together and pray. Children in Phitsanulok, hundreds of miles from the wooded mountains of Chiang Rai, fold thousands of paper cranes for good fortune. Every temple holds vigils. Across Thailand, people feel as if their own son, cousin, brother, or dear friend is trapped inside the cave. Prayers are spoken by a million voices, but they all convey the same message:

Please let them be found. Please let them be alive.

The boys' families have not stopped praying for a moment. They believe what the monk Kruba Boonchum told them: their boys must be alive. But the mood in the rest of camp is at an all-time low. The Thai

Navy SEALs have come. The US Air Force has come. Experts from all over Thailand and all over the world have come. But for the past few days, nothing at the cave has changed. People trudge in. People trudge out, with no news or even a hint that they are any closer to finding the boys.

No one wants to speak out loud what they are thinking, but it's time to start facing the truth: the Wild Boars are most likely dead.

At Sai Tong, Thanet stands in water halfway up his rain boots. Locals have brought in big excavators to widen the holes in the pond even more, allowing water to flow out faster. They have drilled thirteen deep wells that bubble up with brown water, and there are now four super-pumps moving tens of millions of gallons of water each day out of Sai Tong cave.

All that water has to go somewhere, and it floods over 550 acres (2.2 square kilometers) of rice paddies. The farmers are promised by the government that they'll be paid for their ruined fields, but some of them refuse payment. The farmers want to do whatever they can to help the children inside, whom they think of as their own family.

Thanet could sleep for weeks. He and Colonel Singhanat's team have been working at Sai Tong eighteen-hour days for four days in a row. When Thanet finally does leave the work site, his hotel is an hour's drive away. Once in bed, he opens his laptop to send his coworkers back in Bangkok all the water-level data he gathered during the day. He usually doesn't fall asleep until 2:00 a.m., and by 6:00 a.m. it's time to wake up and get right back to Sai Tong.

Water pumping is going full force at the main cave, too. Major Hodges's oil company idea proved to be a good one, and Chevron's industrial pumps are rapidly sucking water out through the mouth of the cave. Just as important, Chevron has donated sturdy pipes that can handle the tremendous suction without collapsing.

On the morning of Sunday, July 1, the skies are clear, and inside the cave there is a striking new development: the water has started to recede. It's difficult to say whether it's the souped-up super-pumps, or

Super-pumps operating at full strength at Sai Tong

the pumping in the main cave, or the halt in rainfall that has made the most difference. Perhaps it's all three. Whatever it is, the British divers are going to take advantage of it.

The water has lowered enough that the Thai SEALs are able to reset their forward base in Chamber 3. It now takes about two hours to slog there on foot from the cave mouth, clambering over slippery, unstable boulders and wading through waist-deep water. But having a base in Chamber 3 means that the divers will have that much less distance to dive. It also means they can have help schlepping in their gear. Crews of SEALs help trek supplies and air tanks to this forward base.

* * *

Rick Stanton (left) and other members of the dive team prepare their gear.

In Chamber 3, Rick and John kit up in all their diving gear and sink into the cloudy water. The visibility is so awful that they can't see more than six inches in front of them. The current is still strong, but it's not as fierce as it was on the first day they dived. They have no idea how much of the cave will still be flooded past Chamber 3, or how far they will have to dive.

They make good progress at first, following the guideline Ben Reymenants laid previously. Vern Unsworth has told them that they'll know when they get to the junction at Sam Yaek because they'll feel a current of warmer, clearer water on their right, coming in from Monk's Series.

True to Vern's description, the two divers find the junction. They turn left and sink down, finding the hole on the left-hand side that leads into the main cave passage. Just past this point is where the Thai SEAL team had to turn back nearly one week ago. Today, Rick and John don't push any farther.

When the divers resurface in Chamber 3 and report the progress they have made, the mood among the rescuers lifts. The Thais have carried a wireless cable into Chamber 3, which means they can send texts instead of relying on the ancient field telephone. A text is sent out to base camp to relay the promising news.

A relieved Governor Narongsak tells the media that hope has returned to the rescue team. "Our officers are smiling and happier than in previous days," he tells journalists.

The forecast shows relatively dry conditions over the next two to three days, but beyond that, rains will likely return. Their window to find the boys is extremely short.

Thai Navy SEALs stand in turbulent water inside Tham Luang.

Thai military and rescue workers hike with sandbags through the forest.

17.
Creating a Diversion

July 1, 2018

THANET'S VOLUNTEER WORK at Sai Tong mostly keeps him away from the bustle of base camp. But on July 1, he makes his way into the chaotic swarm. He is looking for a guy the locals call the Cave Man: Vern Unsworth.

The pumps at the cave mouth and down at Sai Tong are churning full blast, but as long as water is still pouring into the cave at a high rate, diving remains dangerous. Thanet wants to figure out where the water is coming from and stop it. The Cave Man turns out to be the perfect person to ask.

Vern explains to Thanet that if they want to improve the diving conditions, they need to focus on the lowest part of the cave: the junction at Sam Yaek. If they can stop some of the water from flowing in there, the pumps will be more effective.

Most of the water that dumps into Sam Yaek comes from the cave's northern branch — Monk's Series. The last time Vern went to Tham Luang to work on his survey for Monk's Series, he discovered several inlets where water entered that section of the cave. The water that comes in there is warm and relatively clear. This means that unlike the colder water that flows in from unknown underground sources in the south, the water in Monk's Series pours straight into the system from the surface. Vern suggests that Thanet start there.

The next day, Colonel Singhanat's team remains at Sai Tong to continue with the super-pumping, while Thanet goes with a smaller unit of fifty soldiers and local guides to survey the area above Monk's Series. The road curls around the mountain, leading to the small village of Pha Mee.

Thanet has located a creek where he wants to start working, but the roads leading to it are too slippery and his team's trucks nearly careen off the cliff. With no other choice, Thanet and his crew climb out of the trucks and start hiking into the forest. The group hacks its way through the thick vegetation, following streams over slippery, round boulders, lugging heavy supplies with them on their backs.

The local volunteers show them to several streams running swiftly from the recent rains. Geologists at Tham Luang have explained that as the streams run across the top of the mountain, some of the water they carry sinks down into porous limestone underneath. Thanet can see with his own eyes where some streams seem to disappear entirely, dumping into a sinkhole in the ground. On the first day, they find seventeen sinkholes. If they want to lower the water inside the cave, they have to tackle these spots first.

The way they do it is a feat that would impress even Hercules.

Using bamboo poles, ropes, and plastic sheeting, the team creates a barrier between the stream and the mountain so that no water will soak into the stone below. They call these barriers diversion structures because they divert water away so it won't enter the cave. The structure looks a bit like a homemade Slip 'n Slide. Water travels down the Slip 'n Slide, running away from the sinkholes to another part of the mountain where they hope it won't drain into the cave.

In places where streams join and form waterfalls, the Slip 'n Slide

The water diversion team working to divert a mountain stream

Sandbags and pipes are put in place to divert a waterfall. Vines are lashed together to secure one of the pipes.

method doesn't work, so the group brings in long plastic pipes, carrying them on their shoulders through the jungle. Water pours into their galoshes as they stand in the streams, working together to get the pipes in place, where they will divert the water away from the sinkholes.

The team also builds dams using bamboo, rocks, and bags filled with sand and gravel that they dig out of the stream. At first, the people down in base camp are so focused on drilling and searching for alternative

The water diversion team places pipes at a waterfall.

entrances that few are even aware of what Thanet and his crew are doing. Thanet wishes they had better-quality supplies, like proper PVC pipes and high-tech sandbags that fill up with quick-forming concrete as soon as you add water, but they just have to make do with what they've got.

When they can't get pipes, they slice open bamboo poles. When they don't have ropes, they use vines as lashings. The villagers in Pha Mee help by calling for any extra supplies and volunteers that can be spared.

When pipes are unavailable, the water diversion team improvises with thick stalks of bamboo.

It's not until a camera crew from a news station interviews a mud-caked Thanet that his team finally gets the good equipment they need.

Starting on July 2 and continuing throughout the duration of the mission, Thanet and his team carry on with this exhausting and dangerous work, from morning until far past dark. Crews get lost in the black jungle trying to get back to their trucks in the middle of the night. Sprained ankles, pulled muscles, dehydration, bruises, and fungus-covered feet are frequent occurrences. Every day, the medical tent at base camp attends to an injured rescue worker who has hobbled down from the mountain. But the workers' sacrifices will not be for nothing.

Every inch they can lower the water levels inside Tham Luang will make it easier on the divers. And with the window for rescuing the boys growing shorter, the divers will take all the help they can get.

A Thai Navy SEAL battles the ferocious current while carrying a large tank of compressed air.

18.
One Last Try

July 2, 2018

ON THE TENTH DAY the Wild Boars have been missing, Rick and John's goal is to push as far past Sam Yaek as they can. They get ready for the dive ahead, checking their gear and emergency equipment before setting out. The pair carries with them something that is just as important as their diving gear: a mental discipline they have cultivated through decades of cave dives.

That mental strength under pressure is absolutely critical for the long, deep dives that Rick and John tackle. When you are hundreds of yards into a sump, you are so isolated from the basic needs of survival that you may as well be on the surface of the moon. It's no wonder, then, that sump divers seem to possess the same qualities as astronauts: the ability to prepare thoroughly, solve problems quickly, and keep cool in an emergency.

Rick Stanton has a pre-dive ritual that he conducts before he enters the water. It starts with visualizing the upcoming dive, imagining any problems that might arise, and walking through possible solutions.

Rebreathe, Reuse, Recycle

There are two types of breathing equipment available to the divers at Tham Luang: open-circuit equipment and rebreathers. Each type has its advantages and drawbacks.

Our bodies need oxygen to survive, but our lungs can use only a tiny percentage of the oxygen in each breath. Every time you breathe, your body absorbs about 5 percent of the oxygen from each inhale. The other 95 percent gets exhaled along with carbon dioxide. With open-circuit equipment, the exhaled oxygen disappears in streams of bubbles that float to the surface.

A rebreather cuts down on all that waste by recycling the unused oxygen in each breath. The rebreather contains a substance that absorbs the carbon dioxide the diver exhales so they don't breathe it back in. (Inhaling too much carbon dioxide can make you black out — not a good thing when you're swimming through a flooded cave.) The oxygen that the diver doesn't use is passed back through the system to be inhaled on the next breath. A computer monitors the mix of gases in the system and displays the information for the diver.

Rebreathers allow divers to stay underwater far longer and dive much deeper than they can with open-circuit equipment. The moist recycled air from rebreathers also helps keep the diver warmer and more hydrated. But rebreathers have their disadvantages. They are much more complex, with more parts that can fail. And when they do fail, the results can be extreme, such as blackouts or seizures due to the diver getting too little or too much oxygen.

Rick Stanton likes to keep things as simple as possible. The veteran caver, firefighter, and tinkerer designs and builds much of his own equipment (including a thermal vest he cobbled together out of a rubber doormat). The rebreather Rick designed is as streamlined as they come. It doesn't have backup computers for monitoring his oxygen and carbon dioxide levels. Diving without that backup option

A diver wearing rebreather equipment

would make some divers uneasy, but Rick is so in tune with his body that he feels he can detect problems with his equipment as well as any computer.

Some divers at Tham Luang do use rebreathers, but even Rick's simple homemade version is more complicated and bulkier than open-circuit equipment, so Rick and John both choose the open-circuit option.

Rick Stanton and John Volanthen

During his pre-dive ritual, Rick might rehearse how to handle situations like a flooded rebreather or a guideline tangled around his foot, and if problems like these do arise, his mental rehearsals will allow him to stay loose and calm. And when diving a tricky cave like Tham Luang, problems will almost certainly arise. The ability to steadily work through them without panicking is the number one skill a sump diver must have.

As Rick and John slip into the water, their minds are trained on the dive. They aren't thinking back to what they ate for breakfast or what will happen if they don't reach their target destination. They focus on the here and now. That laser focus on the present isn't very different from what Buddhist monks practice during their meditations. In fact, some cave divers talk about diving as a type of meditation, because it's impossible to let your mind wander if you want to stay alive.

Rick and John squeeze past Sam Yaek. Here there is no more guideline to follow, so they lay their own. They have to pause often and tie the line

around boulders so that it doesn't come loose and get carried off in the current. Fighting that current, even with a pair of fins to help with the kicking, makes the going even slower.

Beyond the junction, they come up in a chamber that is relatively dry. They tie off their line and climb out of the water. They believe this is the spot where Vern thinks the boys might be sheltering, but there is no sign of them. They have a few hundred yards of line left, so the two divers get back into the water.

It doesn't take long for them to reach the end of their spool of guideline. They have pushed deep past Sam Yaek and still haven't found anyone. It looks as if they will be returning to base camp without any good news once again.

But when they go to tie off their line, they realize there is an air space above them. Rick surfaces to have a look around. They are in a canal that is only partially filled with water. Rick takes off his mask and sniffs the air.

He smells something awful.

Rick has been preparing himself for the odor of a decomposing dead body. But while the odor he smells is something that most of us would much rather not encounter, it fills him with relief: the smell of human feces.

Cables snake through the passages of Tham Luang. A meter stick measures the current water levels.

19.
"Brilliant"

July 2, 2018

DEEP IN THAM LUANG, the Wild Boars are doing what they have been doing for the past three days: digging at the walls of the room that has become their tiny home. They are talking with each other, trying to keep their minds off their hunger, when suddenly Coach Ek stops and holds still.

"Did you hear something?"

The team has become used to hearing things in the darkness. When the boys meditate, sometimes they hear dogs barking or chickens squawking. They have even heard the whir of helicopter blades. They are so deep under the surface that these sounds can only be illusions. The constant echo of water dripping onto stone can play tricks on one's mind. Cavers who spend long periods underground sometimes hear what they think are the voices or footsteps of their friends just behind them, only to find there is no one nearby.

But this time, Coach Ek is sure that he heard a man's voice. He tells the others to be quiet.

Yes! There it is again — a voice and the sound of splashing.

The group moves down toward the water. Mix holds the flashlight, and Coach Ek tells him to hurry down to the shore.

"Don't let them pass us!" he says.

Their hill is so high that Coach fears that whoever is in the water may sink down again and swim right past without seeing them.

Mix is timid, so Adul takes the flashlight and waves it down at the water.

"Hello?" he calls out.

He hears an answer, but he can't tell what they say. And he still can't see the speaker's face.

Finally, two heads emerge into the beam of his flashlight.

Adul is taken aback. The faces bobbing above the water aren't Thai; they belong to two white men.

"Is anyone there?" one of the men calls.

It takes Adul a second to register that they're speaking *English*. Adul has learned English in school, and the pastor at his church has also been teaching him. But the words come slowly to his lips. His mind is sluggish from so many days of hunger and darkness.

Adul knows he has to say something.

"Hello!" he calls back in English.

"Are you OK?" asks the man. Thankfully, he's speaking slowly.

Adul thinks a moment. They've been trapped in a cave for ten days without any food, but other than that, they're pretty OK.

"Yes, I am OK," he answers.

The man asks, *"How many of you?"*

"Thirteen," answers Adul.

"Brilliant."

Coach Ek, who doesn't speak English, asks the boys nearest to him, "What are they saying? Does anyone know? Who here speaks English?"

Thi reminds him that Bew knows a little English.

"Please translate!" pleads Coach Ek.

Photo taken from the helmet video camera of the British divers when the Wild Boars were found

"Calm down," Bew tells him in Thai. "I can't translate and listen at the same time! Oh, great. Now I can't catch up."

The team is realizing that everything they have prayed for is really happening. Feelings of relief and happiness rush over them fast. It's such a contrast to the slow, dark days they have been enduring. The whole scene feels dreamlike. After ten days by themselves, here are two more human beings, people from the outside who have come to help them.

All the boys are wondering the same two things: Do we get to leave the cave now? And do these guys have any food tucked inside their wet suits?

Sadly, the answer to the first question is no.

The first man explains in short, choppy sentences why they can't leave the cave: *"No, not today. Just two of us. We have to dive."*

The second diver says, *"We are coming. It's OK. Many people are coming."*

The first diver adds, *"Many, many people. We are the first. Many people come."*

That's awesome, but the boys want to know when they get to leave this stinking cave.

"What day?" Adul asks them, meaning what day will they finally see the sky again.

"Tomorrow."

The men start talking quickly to each other. Then one of them holds up his hands and says, *"One week . . . uh, Monday. You have been here for ten days."*

He obviously doesn't realize that the boys have a watch and know exactly how long they've been here.

Meanwhile, Bew has remembered his English. *"Hungry! Hungry!"* he says, and others join in the chant.

"We are hungry," Adul repeats.

"I know," says the man. *"I understand."*

That sounds like a no to the question of snacks tucked inside wet suits.

The men move closer and tell the boys that they are coming out of the water, up the slope. They're wearing full wet suits and tanks on their backs. They look like clumsy ducks in their long flippers, and it's not easy for them to climb up the slippery rocks. When one of them stumbles, Adul reaches out and asks if he needs any help.

"No, it's OK," says the man. He just needs them to move back a bit. The team makes room for the two men on the sand.

"Did you tell them we're hungry?" one of the boys whispers to Adul.

"Yes, yes, I told them already," answers Adul.

There is no food today, but there will be tomorrow. The men explain that Thai Navy SEALs will come to them the next day and bring food and a doctor with them.

"Where do you come from?" asks Adul.

"England. The UK," answer the men.

England? Seriously? The boys believed that they would be found someday, but the last thing they expected was that two men in diving gear — all the way from England — would be the ones to find them.

"I am very happy," Adul says to the Englishmen, words that don't begin to convey the overwhelming joy they all feel.

The men seem to understand anyway. And maybe they don't have the words to fully express what they are feeling either.

"We are happy, too," they say.

Before Rick and John depart, they leave the boys with the only thing they have to give them: flashlights. The boys thank them, and then they each wrap their arms around the men in a hug. This is an unusual show of affection, and it carries a real meaning. Thai people are very affectionate with loved ones, and it's common for friends and family to hug and hold hands, but hugging a stranger—especially a foreign stranger—is not the norm. By hugging Rick and John, the boys are not just showing how grateful they are to be saved. These two men are no longer strangers. They have become like family.

The divers promise they will come back. As they dip back down below the water, Rick and John refocus on the harrowing dive ahead of them. There is one thought they won't allow themselves to dwell on until they are safely on dry ground again. The dive through the cave was even more difficult than they predicted, and the boys they saw were so emaciated—like walking skeletons. They have made a promise to return to the Wild Boars, and they aren't worried about keeping that promise. What they don't know is how in the world the boys who just hugged them are going to get out.

Later, John Volanthen will speak his grim thoughts aloud: "Alive in a cave and alive outside a cave are two very different things."

The Wild Boars' families are elated at learning that their sons have been found.

20.
Now What?

July 3, 2018

GOVERNOR NARONGSAK is with his staff in the makeshift mission command center, a park headquarters building just uphill from the cave, when his phone rings. As soon as he finishes the call, he bolts out the door. He finds Admiral Apakorn and hugs him! Volunteers on-site hear about this, and they wonder. The mission commander and the commander of the Thai Navy SEALs are *hugging*? Could this actually be good news?

Within minutes the world finds out just how good the news is. Rick and John have emerged from the cave with precious treasure: a video of their encounter with the team, showing all thirteen of them alive and well. The boys' families are beside themselves with joy. The video quickly circulates around the campground outside the cave and is posted online, where it goes viral. All over Thailand — all over the globe — the video of the thin boys scooching down the slope plays on constant repeat.

The story of the Wild Boars is an international sensation. The soccer team everyone thought was dead has been found alive! It's practically a miracle. People all over the world who are hungry for some happy news are riveted by this feel-good story.

But even as the elation at finding the boys spreads across the province, the country, and the world, the rescue team on-site at Tham Luang holds stone-faced meetings. Sure, they found the boys alive and well, but now what? The Wild Boars are two miles (2.5 kilometers) deep into Tham Luang and almost half a mile (600 meters) below the surface. Every option for rescuing them has problems.

The search for alternate entrances has so far proved futile. The military, the police, and the volunteer bird's nest collectors have scoured every crevice of the mountain for even the smallest possible entrance and have found nothing. It seems that the only way into and out of the cave is through its mouth.

Since they can't find an alternative opening into the cave, how about making their own? Before the boys were found, the major obstacle to drilling into the mountain was picking a location. But even now that the rescuers know where the Wild Boars are, drilling is still not feasible. For one thing, it's no small task to bring the drilling equipment to Tham Luang. When the Chilean miners were rescued in 2010, they were located in a place that had easy access to a road. In order to drill into the Nang Non mountains, the drilling rig will have to be lowered into place by a helicopter. Teams of workers have already started clearing a landing zone in the jungle for this purpose, but that's not the only problem.

Geologists working with the US Air Force have taken ultrasound readings of the area. They report that the thinnest spot they can find to drill into is 650 feet (200 meters) thick. It will take two days just to bore a hole four to six inches (10 to 15 centimeters) wide through the limestone. It could take weeks, maybe even months, to drill a hole big enough to extract a person. With more rain on the way, they don't have time to get this in place.

Another option is to drain the sumps. If they could somehow pump out enough water from the cave to create small pockets of air at the top of each passage, then the boys could be floated out on rafts or life preservers. But the current pumping operation is already going at full steam. Water is chugging out of Sai Tong, flooding thousands of surrounding rice farms. Thanet and his crews have just started building diversion structures on the mountain, but it's doubtful that they can lower the water levels enough to eliminate diving altogether. When it rains again, the pumps will likely be overwhelmed once more.

Another option is to simply wait it out.

For some, this seems like the least risky option. Nang Non has been a dry cave before, and it will be a dry cave again after the rainy season is over. Sure, the kids are uncomfortable, perched in that desolate place, but they are miraculously healthy, and now that divers can bring them food, they will slowly gain their strength back. They are also no longer alone.

As soon as Rick and John emerge from their trip to what has now been labeled Chamber 9, a group of six Thai SEALs and a Thai army doctor named Pak Loharachun prepare a supply-delivery dive. Without telling the British divers or the US Air Force, the SEALs don their diving gear, pack energy gels and medicines into their wet suits and dry bags, and set off into the cave.

The original plan had been to dive in, deliver supplies, give the Wild Boars a medical check, and then dive back out. But without cave-diving experience or the rebreathers that cave divers often use, the SEALs end up using most of their air supply on the way in. The current is much stronger than they predicted. It takes a lot of energy—and too many breaths—to fight it.

At one point, Dr. Pak finds himself in a crisis when he loses both his regulator and his hold of the guideline. Panic begins to seize him. Only by focusing on thoughts of his family and his former teachers is he able to calm down enough to find them both again. By the time the group reaches Chamber 9, they have only enough air supply to send three of the six SEALs back to the entrance.

A Thai Navy SEAL holds the guideline as he dives. This thick climbing rope was used as guideline in the sumps between the cave entrance and Sam Yaek. Beyond that point, Rick and John laid their own line, which was likely thinner.

Even then, it takes the returning SEALs much longer than they anticipated to get back out. It had taken the British divers about an hour and a half to dive between Chambers 3 and 9 — and a little less time to return with the current. When the SEALs finally return to Chamber 3, twenty-three hours have passed since they departed. Those waiting in Chamber 3 cheer with relief when they see the headlamps breach the surface. They were sure their comrades had died.

Extra tanks could be brought to Dr. Pak and the three remaining SEALs to allow them to make the return dive later. But they choose to stay in Chamber 9, putting their own lives at risk. If the water rises, diving will become impossible, and the men will be trapped with the boys.

One SEAL later explained his decision: "I told myself that I would go into the cave, and if the boys didn't come out I wouldn't come out either. I would stay there as long as it took."

The Wild Boars now have food and medical supplies. Apart from some cuts on their feet and legs, the boys have no injuries. But the wet, dirty environment of a cave wreaks havoc on the skin, where any scrape or blister can become easily infected. Dr. Pak spreads iodine on their wounds and monitors their health.

Being in constant darkness weakens the immune system, so it's surprising that the boys aren't sicker when they are found. Night has developed a slight chest cold, and everyone is chilled to the bone. They are given lightweight silvery space blankets, which look like big sheets of aluminum foil. The reflective surface of these blankets traps the body's heat, warming the boys much more effectively than cloth.

All of the boys were very malnourished when they were found. Now they finally get to have food, though it's not exactly the stuff of their dreams.

The boys have been dreaming of Kentucky Fried Chicken, fried rice and omelets, and gai phat kaphrao — chicken stir-fried with garlic, basil, and peppers and served with rice and a fried egg. Their mouths watered at the thought that they would finally be able to taste these dishes. But when a person goes without eating for a long time, they have to be reintroduced to foods slowly. The first food the Thai SEALs bring to the boys is something very simple: a high-energy gel packed with sugars and nutrients. The sugary goo is typically used by marathon runners to give them a quick boost of calories in the middle of a race. It's perfect here because packets of it can be swum back to the boys in the divers' wet suits.

The boys are allowed one indulgence in the early days after they are found: a few nibbles of a Beng-Beng candy bar, something they have all been craving.

On July 4, Rick and John make another supply dive back to Chamber 9. This time they bring MREs, or Meals Ready to Eat, which are used by the

US military when troops are in the field with no ability to cook for themselves. Each meal is about 1,250 calories and has an entrée (such as beef stew or spaghetti), a side dish, dessert, and even hot sauce.

The Thai SEALs and the doctor are doing more than just physically taking care of the team. Their presence helps the boys feel safe and less homesick. Halfway up the hill in Chamber 9, the SEALs carve out a flat ledge for the boys to rest on so they don't have to climb all the way to the top of the slope. Here, they play games with the boys, setting up makeshift chess and checkers games using rocks and a playing board drawn into the sand. Even though the boys have been through a harrowing experience, the SEALs never let them win a chess game. Far from feeling defeated, the boys relish having something to train their mind on besides digging and drinking water. One of the SEALs in particular is a funny wisecracker. Knowing how uncomfortable and cold the boys were, he gave them his clothes and thermal blankets. This left him in nothing but his underwear, which led to lots of laughter and teasing, mostly by him.

Even though the four Thais who remain in Chamber 9 with the boys hadn't planned on staying, the Wild Boars are grateful to have them. The boys had misunderstood what Rick and John told them when they said "Tomorrow." The team thought it meant they would be taken out of the cave the very next day, but the Englishmen had only meant that people would return and supplies would be delivered. The disappointment of having to stay another day, and another, and another inside Tham Luang might have been unbearable if the four men weren't there to boost morale.

As it is, the boys are all in amazingly good spirits. They are polite and courteous to all of the people helping them. When they eat, they always clean up after themselves, throwing their trash away and keeping their area tidy.

The British divers in particular seem stunned that the kids are so upbeat. The team has been stuck underground for ten days with no food and no contact with the outside world, using the bathroom just a few yards away from where they have to sleep, but they aren't whining or complaining. Instead there are smiles. "Really strong composure," diver Jason Mallinson marveled later. "Real mental strength from them, which was surprising considering their ages."

The British divers may have been a little misguided by the Wild Boars' smiling faces. Thailand's tourism slogan is the "Land of Smiles," and visitors to the country often say that people here smile more than most. But in Thailand, smiling isn't something you do solely to express happiness. Thai people may smile during an argument, or when they've just lost their wallet, or when they get into a fender bender. A smile is a way to make the people around you feel comfortable, to keep the situation cool, and to keep cool yourself.

It's not surprising that the Wild Boars smile for their rescuers. They trust the men who found them. They are happy and grateful to be found, and it would be bad manners to complain or whine. But make no mistake: the boys are desperate to get out of that cave.

The SEALs record a video of the Wild Boars in Chamber 9 and post it to their Facebook page. The boys sit shoulder to shoulder, the silvery heat-trapping blankets wrapped around them like cloaks. They smile and wai — pressing their hands together in front of their faces — and some give the two-fingered "peace" sign. But despite the smiles, they look exhausted, weak, and so much thinner than the athletic soccer players who first ventured into the cave. They need to come home.

But for the moment, no one knows how to make that happen. It seems pretty much impossible.

Volunteers and workers at Tham Luang base camp

21.
The Get-It-Done Crew

July 3–4, 2018

DESPITE THE UNCERTAINTY over how to get them out, finding the boys sends a surge of energy throughout base camp. No one feels the shift more than the volunteers who have been on-site since the first day the boys went missing. The mountain now swells with ten thousand people: rescue workers, divers, military personnel, monks, medics, and the scores of volunteers supporting them. Some merely want to be seen being part of the Tham Luang phenomenon, but most are eager to help in any way they can.

A dedicated team of local Thais has been posted at the cave for the past ten days, doing all manner of random jobs vital to the mission—even when that mission seemed utterly hopeless. Most don't report to any one organization but have organized themselves into a makeshift crew that sees what needs to be done and does it without waiting to be asked.

From the moment the operation began, the team working inside the cave has needed a lot of stuff—rescue equipment, food, water, and clothing—and they've needed it fast. Finding all the stuff and getting it to Tham Luang falls on the shoulders of Chaiyon "Ay" Srisamoot and Anuphas "Noi" Patisen, two local leaders from Mae Sai. In the early days, before the governor declares the situation an emergency, there is no government money to buy anything. So Ay and Noi have to call around and ask for donations. The people of Mae Sai come through in droves.

Ay sets up a line of tents outside the cave and organizes the donated items: flashlights, headlamps, every size of battery, ropes and carabiners, medicines, bandages, and mosquito spray. When the military first arrived at Tham Luang, they had no idea how long they would be there and had packed only enough clean clothes for two days. So Ay collects donations of shirts, pants, socks, underwear, even boots. He also collects lots of food for the hungry Navy SEALs: cups of instant noodles, chicken stock, snacks, water, and energy drinks. The tents become like a tiny outdoor department store (where everything is free). And if the tent-store doesn't have it, Ay's crew will find it.

The SEALs have shifts working twenty-four hours a day. Odd requests come at odd hours. When someone needs a hair dryer at 3:00 a.m. to use on some quick-setting glue, Ay's crew sends someone out in the middle of the night to knock on friends' doors and bring it back. When Ay can't find the waterproof headlamps the Navy SEALs need anywhere in Mae Sai, he calls friends in Myanmar, who bring the items across the border.

If anything is too hard to find, the crew puts a call out on social media. Through Facebook and other apps, the request gets beamed beyond Mae Sai to the surrounding provinces and even all the way to Bangkok. When the SEALs request the energy gel packs that will be the boys' first food in ten days, Ay can't find any in the area. Within hours of posting about the need online, he is sending a friend off to the Chiang Rai airport to pick up a box of gel packs flown in from the capital city.

As the rescue goes on, the crew sets up a collections depot to handle the huge flow of donations. Noi's blue GM pickup truck becomes a frequent sight, zipping through town to gather supplies and bring them to

Ay, on the right, with volunteers who are cooking meals for the rescue team

base camp. When the roads leading into Tham Luang become congested with soldiers and journalists, the only vehicles that can get through are motorcycles. Soon anyone who lives in the area with a motorbike becomes part of the crew, ferrying supplies and people up to the cave mouth, without asking to be repaid for their gasoline or their time.

Getting enough food for everyone on-site is a constant challenge. The Navy SEALs not only need protein-rich meals; they also need food that can be carried into a wet, muddy cave and not spoil. Ruthaiwan "Nok" Padisen, a ranger with the parks department, makes it her responsibility to find and pack the SEALs' food. Every day she wakes up before dawn to wrap pork and sticky rice into vacuum-sealed packets. Out of consideration for the Muslim Navy SEALs, she also prepares food packets without pork. Each day she produces hundreds of packets and delivers them to

Park ranger Nok, who packaged meals for the Thai Navy SEALs throughout the mission

the cave entrance. It's so much work that she goes home only to take a shower before hurrying back to base camp to start again. Throughout the entire mission, Nok sleeps little more than a few hours a night.

Taking care of the British diving team falls on the shoulders of Tik and her friend Busakorn "Laa" Patisen. They drive Rick and John wherever they need to go and make sure they have all the equipment they need. Worried that the British divers can't stomach the traditional spicy Thai food the SEALs eat, Tik and Laa drive into town every day to purchase Western food, like pizza and hamburgers.

As for the volunteers themselves, many have had to scrounge up whatever food they can find. But once Rick and John find the Wild Boars, all of that changes. Suddenly, good food arrives at base camp. The king of Thailand has been monitoring the situation at Tham Luang. He sends food trucks to cook everyone hot, fresh meals. He also sends two thousand raincoats, which the rescuers sorely need. They have been slogging through the mud for days, and most people have the blisters and rotten feet to prove it.

Scores of other volunteers arrive and set up big cookstoves in front of the cave. For the duration of the rescue, the smell of sizzling garlic and freshly brewed coffee wafts through camp at all hours. Muslim cooks come to make delicious halal meals (food that is prepared according to Islamic dietary law), which they hand out freely to anyone regardless of religion. Volunteers handle the mountains of dirty laundry. Massage therapists work on aching backs and feet. Still more volunteers pick up trash and clean toilets. No one is paid a dime.

When journalists ask them why they are at Tham Luang, working so hard and for free, the volunteers have a hard time coming up with an answer. For them, it seems like a no-brainer. If they can help, why would they stay away? This is Thailand. People take care of one another here.

From left to right: Ay, Noi, Laa, and Tik, volunteers who worked on-site at Tham Luang throughout the rescue

Divers wade through waist-deep water at Tham Luang

22.
Panic

July 5, 2018

THERE IS ONE LAST OPTION for getting the boys out of Tham Luang. But it is so dangerous that it is considered by many to be the option of very last resort.

The boys could dive their way out of the cave.

Rick Stanton and John Volanthen have already put out the request to send more rescue divers to Thailand. If they do end up diving the boys out through the flooded passages, they will need help. And not just any-one will do.

They need divers with both extreme sump-diving experience and res-cue experience, who will share the workload without complaints, will keep their cool under pressure, and can handle the emotional burden of having a child's life in their hands.

Most importantly, Rick and John need to work with divers that they know and trust. Cave divers choose their partners with even more care than they select their diving equipment. Having the right partner underwater can literally mean the difference between life and death.

Quick-thinking divers have saved their partners' lives by dragging them out of rip currents, recognizing a broken oxygen gauge, or cutting them out of tangled guidelines.

Some of the first divers to be flown out to join the team at Tham Luang are Jason Mallinson and Chris Jewell. Along with Rick and John, Jason and Chris are right there at the top of the list of the world's best cave divers. Jason has dived to the ends of some of the longest and most remote tunnels on our planet. And Jason and Chris were both part of a team that just a few years prior had undertaken a weeks-long expedition to dive the deepest cave in the Western Hemisphere.

Jason is well known for being cool under pressure and for surviving plenty of near-death situations underwater. His first thought on learning about the team's position and the diving conditions?

These kids are not going to make it out.

The news media at this time seems obsessed with reporting one detail that is actually untrue: that none of the boys know how to swim. Maybe it adds drama to the rescue mission to think about non-swimmers having to dive out through the cave. But Jason Mallinson knows that it wouldn't matter if the boys were Olympic swimmers. Their biggest obstacle to a dive rescue isn't swimming.

It's panic.

Cave divers control every step of their dive, planning out even the smallest details. But panic is the one element of diving that no one can plan for. "Panic is a knife's edge," says veteran cave diver Bill Stone. "On one side of the blade, you are rational; you can make good decisions and problem-solve. But as soon as you fall to that other side, and you let panic take over, it's almost impossible to bring yourself out of it." Especially underwater.

Even experienced divers have succumbed to panic. Something triggers it — perhaps losing the guideline or having a mask flood with water. Perhaps it's getting stuck in a narrow squeeze or entangled in a line or reaching for your regulator only to find that the valve on your air tank was left open and you have much less air than you thought. Sometimes it's nothing at all. Your mind can trick you into thinking something is malfunctioning or going wrong when everything is perfectly normal.

Once panic sets in, your body's first response is to heave rapid, full breaths. Underwater, this is the worst response, because the faster you breathe, the quicker you burn through the air in your tank. Panic can also make you act strangely. You might freeze up, hugging the cave wall in a statue-like state, rather than trying to search for the way out. Divers who have panicked have swum frantically in different directions or taken off swimming in the wrong direction entirely. Panic can induce you to do things you would never do under normal circumstances, like pull off your face mask or yank your regulator out of your mouth.

How would a child who had never even put on a face mask before react? They would almost certainly panic during the dive out. That panic would be lethal for them and likely lethal for their rescuer as well. The risk of panic is one of the main reasons people are looking so hard for alternatives to a dive rescue.

The space exploration company SpaceX has offered their services to the BCRC, and they quickly begin the design and assembly of a tiny submersible capsule. Perhaps the boys could crouch in the capsule, breathing air, and be pushed and guided through the flooded passages by the divers. But ultimately, the capsule idea is abandoned because it can't make the tight twists and turns of the cavern's innards and has no way of monitoring the gas mixture for the passenger inside.

The Thai leadership is leaning toward leaving the boys inside the cave until the end of the rainy season. While waiting sounds dismal, it seems less dangerous than trying to dive the boys out. After all, the kids seem to be doing fairly well right now. And the SEALs have had some success at getting food and medicine back to them. If they can just sit tight for a bit longer, maybe they can walk out of Tham Luang on their own feet.

In the meantime, the supply dives are continuing. When Jason

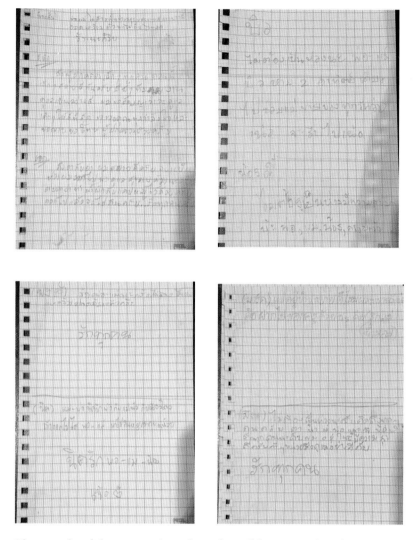

Photographs of the notes written from the Wild Boars to their families

Mallinson dives back to deliver food to the boys, he has the sudden idea to let them write short notes for their parents on his waterproof writing pad. Jason knows the options for rescuing the boys are dwindling, and he has the sad thought that these notes could very well be the boys' last words to their parents.

As wretched as their situation is, the boys all tell their parents not to worry about them:

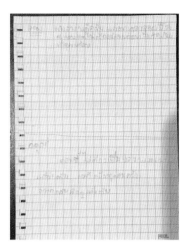

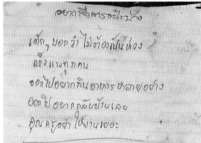

Don't worry, Mom and Dad. I have been gone for two weeks, but when I get out, I will go help Mom sell things at the shop. I will hurry to get there. — Bew

Don't worry about me. I miss everyone. The Navy SEALs are taking good care of me. — Mix

Mom, you're at home. How are you? I'm fine. Can you let my teachers know? — Mark

I love Dad and Mom. Don't worry about me. I'm safe. I love you all. — Pong

The parents cherish the letters from their sons and send back encouraging notes of their own.

The parents worry about Coach Ek, who wrote to them in his letter: "To all the parents, know the kids are fine. . . . I promise I will take care of them as best I can. Thank you to everyone who has come to help. I am very sorry to the parents." They send him notes back, reassuring him that they don't blame him at all: "Coach Ek, we trust you, so don't

Thanet Natisri with the capsule designed by SpaceX

blame yourself. We want you to understand that what happened is not your fault. We love you and want to thank you for taking care of our boys even though you could lose your own life. We would never blame you. We pray for you and the kids to come out safely."

Sending the messages back and forth is a happy moment for the kids and their families, who haven't seen each other or spoken in almost two weeks. But along with the sweet letters, the British divers also bring worrying news from Chamber 9. With the SEALs and Dr. Pak now in the chamber with the boys, more people are inhaling oxygen and exhaling carbon dioxide into the small room. Air-quality meters reveal that oxygen levels in the chamber have dropped from the normal 21 percent to around 15 percent. Even healthy adults find it hard to work or move around when oxygen drops below 19 percent. Less than 12 percent causes people to gasp for breath and their lips to turn blue. Anything lower than 10 percent, and people pass out and can die.

The Thais have a plan to address the dropping oxygen levels: they will pump oxygen from the outside all the way back to Chamber 9. The Thai Navy SEALs begin carrying bulky coils of flexible tubing into Tham Luang. Major Charles Hodges is dismayed to see the oxygen tube being carried in. Only days before this, his team had worked doggedly alongside the SEALs to clear out the awful tangle of cords, guidelines, and power cables that twisted through the cave. Now there will just be more stuff gunking up the passages, making diving more difficult.

Frustrated by the plan and by the lack of communication, Major Hodges decides to pull his team out of the cave on July 6 to take a much-needed rest.

That same night, he gets a call from base camp that tragedy has struck inside Tham Luang.

Pump hoses and tubes being carried up the steps that lead into Tham Luang

Thai Navy SEALs carry oxygen tanks into Tham Luang.

23.

A Tragic Loss

July 5–6, 2018

THE ROYAL THAI NAVY SEALS have impressed everyone at Tham Luang with their stamina and fighting spirit. They seem to work tirelessly, though by now—going on Day 13 of the rescue—they are surely exhausted. When they sleep at all, they snatch only a few hours inside the cave. They carry heavy loads of supplies and air tanks, trekking back and forth between the entrance and the forward base in Chamber 3. The SEALs' rallying cry, a deep belly-chant of "HOOYAH!" energizes everyone who hears it. Even the lack of proper cave-diving equipment or training doesn't stop them from tackling Tham Luang's sumps.

Not every Thai Navy SEAL at Tham Luang is on active duty. Almost fifty members of the SEAL team on-site have come out of retirement to support the rescue mission. Even in retirement, the SEALs remain a close-knit band of brothers, often getting together to keep up their training. Once the news of the missing soccer team reached them, many put everything aside and rushed to Mae Sai.

Saman Gunan (on the left, in blue) with other divers and members of the Thai Navy SEALs

One of the SEALs to come out of retirement was thirty-eight-year-old Saman Gunan. Saman was working as a security guard at the international airport in Bangkok when he heard about the situation at Tham Luang. An accomplished triathlete and long-distance biker, Saman knew his skills could be of use to the SEALs. As he boarded a plane bound for northern Thailand, he recorded a video for his wife and family. "May luck be on our side," he said as he climbed the stairs to the plane. "Let's bring the boys home."

Late at night on July 5, Saman and his dive partner set off into Tham Luang, carrying canisters of air. They are "staging" the tanks, a common practice for long cave dives. They will place extra tanks of air at dry areas in key locations so that divers can replenish their supplies if they run out. The Navy SEALs carry three air tanks with them for their own personal use, and they pull three additional tanks along behind them.

The SEALs stationed in Chamber 3 notice that Saman and his dive partner have been gone too long—almost fifteen hours. When Saman's partner finally emerges, he is pulling a lifeless Saman behind him. The other SEALs rush to revive him, but it's too late.

No one knows exactly what triggered the drowning. Saman was physically fit and had a lot of open-water diving experience, but the narrow passages would confound even the most experienced sump divers. The addition of the clunky coils of oxygen tubing could have made getting through the sumps even more dangerous. The conditions are so perilous that while the cave divers are sorrowful to hear of Saman's death, they aren't shocked that Tham Luang has claimed a life.

The Navy SEALs are like a family, and Saman's death sends a tremor of sadness through base camp. But though Saman's comrades are gutted by his loss, they also remind themselves that they still have a mission to finish. No one wants Saman's death to be in vain. If anything, losing him gives the rescue team a grim determination to carry out the rest of the operation.

The rescuers at Tham Luang will need every ounce of that determination. The weather report for the upcoming weekend is not in their favor.

More rain is on the way.

A memorial to Saman Gunan

Mission commander Governor Narongsak speaks during a press conference at Tham Luang.

24.
Risking It All

July 6, 2018

SAMAN GUNAN'S DEATH triggers two very different responses among the rescuers at base camp.

The British divers see the loss as proof that it's not possible to keep the boys in the cave until the rainy season is over. If the boys stay inside, there will need to be many more supply dives to restock food, which would put even more divers' lives at risk. Vern Unsworth insists that even though the rainy season ends in November, the cave still remains flooded until at least January. That means the boys would have to wait six months to get out.

Along with Chris Jewell and Jason Mallinson, more expert cave divers have arrived at base camp from all over the world, giving Rick and John the assistance they would need to carry out a dive rescue. This would be extremely risky, but they must get the children out of the cave as soon as possible. The oxygen levels in Chamber 9 are dipping dangerously low. Unless they dive, "they'll be bringing out thirteen dead bodies," Vern says gravely.

Human Responses to Levels of Oxygen Concentration	
Oxygen Level	**Body's Responses**
21%	• Normal
15–19%	• Unable to exert strenuous energy • Impaired coordination
10–12%	• Breathing rate increases. • Lips turn blue. • Judgment is impaired.
8–10%	• Fainting • Unconsciousness
6–8%	• Recovery is possible if normal oxygen levels are restored within 4–5 minutes. • Death occurs within 8 minutes.

By contrast, Saman's death proves to the Thai leadership just how impossible a dive rescue will be. If a strapping triathlete Navy SEAL with scuba experience can perish during a dive in Tham Luang, how in the world can they expect twelve underfed kids and their coach to make it out? For the Thais, a dive is simply too deadly. Two days earlier, Governor Narongsak had given a press briefing and promised all of Thailand that the boys would be brought out using a "zero risk" option. Diving is the opposite of zero risk.

The Thais are also heartened by what they view as a vital piece of information. The boys have told the SEALs that they've heard dogs barking and chickens clucking, and that at one point they could hear the buzz of helicopter blades overhead. This must mean that the team is near some sort of shaft that allows sound to reach them from the surface. The rescuers just need to be patient and work to find this shaft. It might take a little drilling, but why take the chance of dragging the boys out underwater when they could just lift them up to the surface?

On the morning of July 6, Thanet Natisri and Colonel Singhanat get set to board a helicopter that will survey the mountainside to find more places to divert water. As they wait for the trucks that will take them to the chopper base, they run into Vern Unsworth and some members of the British Cave Rescue Council. They learn that the British team has tried to urge the Thais to give them permission to perform a dive rescue, but they failed to persuade anyone.

Thanet is frustrated by the Thai leadership's refusal. He agrees that a dive rescue is the only option at this point. He knows from talking to Vern Unsworth that the kids are so far underground that it's impossible for them to have heard any sounds from the surface. If there were any shafts that break through into the cave, Vern would know about them. The boys are just hearing things.

Thanet's team has been battling against the water for days now. They have managed to beat it back, but only because everyone has been working themselves nearly to death and because the skies have been clear. Thanet thinks about the dams and makeshift Slip 'n Slides his team has painstakingly put in place above Monk's Series. The structures are holding now, but a heavy rain could wash it all away.

If the water levels rise again in Tham Luang, diving will become impossible. The British divers made a grueling trip the day before to stock Chamber 9 with a hundred military-style vacuum-packed meals. If the boys are going to wait out the rainy season, they will need a minimum of 1,800 meals. That means eighteen days of restocking trips.

The rains will not hold out for eighteen days. Once the floodwaters rise, supply divers won't be able to make the trip back, and the food the boys do have will quickly dwindle. The water could even rise so high that it would flood the slope the boys are sheltered on. In that case, the children would not survive one day, let alone the weeks it would take to set up a successful drilling operation.

Even without a catastrophic flood, the oxygen levels in Chamber 9 are too low to sustain the seventeen people now crowded there. After Saman's death, the SEALs decided it was too risky to try pumping in extra oxygen, and the tube was removed. The boys are pretty healthy at the moment, but how much longer can they last without the proper amount of oxygen, food, and medical care? What if one of the children develops an infection? The moist, dirty environment of a cave is a breeding ground for bacteria. Thanet shudders at the thought of the boys watching their teammates fall ill and die one by one as the waters rise around them.

Even though the British team and the Thai government officials are camped out in the very same parking lot with each other, there is a massive gap in communication. It doesn't seem that the Thai leadership knows about the dropping oxygen levels in Chamber 9, or how difficult it will be to stock the boys with enough supplies to ride out the rainy season.

Thanet speaks to Colonel Singhanat. The two men decide that they have to get all this information to the Thai officials and try to change their minds. They first go to Singhanat's commanders in the Thai army. The answer from the army is to stick with the plan of keeping the children inside. Any change from that decision has to be approved by the Thai Navy SEALs.

At this point, Thanet and Singhanat have hit a wall. In Thai culture, status and rank are important. Younger and less experienced people are expected to show respect to their elders. A young restaurant owner with no military rank or title can't just waltz up to a military commander and start giving him advice. Singhanat is an officer in the army — a completely different branch of the military from the SEALs. He would be stepping way outside his duties to cross over and speak with the SEAL commander, and his whole career could be at risk if he tries. His

Seated at the table from left to right: Vern Unsworth, Rob Harper, Thanet Natisri, Woranan "Tik" Ratrawiphakkun, and Colonel Singhanat

orders are clear: Do not step out of your lane. Do not question your superiors.

But Colonel Singhanat decides he has to take the chance. In the SEALs' camp, Thanet and Singhanat find SEAL commander Rear Admiral Apakorn. They bring along an American caver named Josh Morris, who lives in Thailand and speaks fluent Thai. Josh has been volunteering as a translator for the British team. Colonel Singhanat approaches Admiral Apakorn with great humility and politeness and requests just a few moments to speak with him. The commander agrees to a brief conversation.

"Brother, thank you for hearing us out," says Colonel Singhanat. "We would like to provide you with some information we have learned from the British divers and the international team."

Singhanat, Thanet, and Josh quickly update Admiral Apakorn with every bit of information they have. As the rear admiral listens, his face becomes more and more serious. When the men are finished making their case, Apakorn confides that his SEALs have been working to the point of exhaustion, and he worries about how much longer they can keep up their backbreaking efforts. He agrees to use his authority to support a dive rescue.

He says that in the evening all the high-level Thai officials will gather in the War Room in base camp to discuss the path forward. Thailand's minister of the interior, Anupong Paochinda, will be there. The minister of the interior oversees all the governors of every province in Thailand and reports directly to the prime minister himself. If they can convince Minister Paochinda, then they should be able to get permission to go

Rescuers gather around a map of the Tham Luang cave system

forward with the dive rescue. But they must have a solid plan to present. Every detail must be thought out, because if there are any cracks in the plan, the Thai leadership will think it's too risky and will back out.

Thanet, Colonel Singhanat, and Josh thank Admiral Apakorn and then hurry across base camp to where the US Air Force squadron is stationed. Thanet has already met Major Charles Hodges and his divemaster, Sergeant Derek Anderson, and he admires how they conduct themselves. They are professional and straightforward but also very respectful and even-tempered. If anyone can make a solid case for diving the children out, it's them. But will they be able to design an airtight plan in time for the meeting?

The Americans tell Thanet that not only do they have a solid plan for the rescue, but they had it a couple of days ago. Sergeant Anderson knows that the success of a mission depends on managing every detail. He has been talking with the British divers, and they have designed a thorough rescue plan with backup for anything that could possibly go wrong. This plan is as strong as it's going to get. They're ready to present it anytime to anyone.

The meeting is set for that night at 10:00 p.m. They will have one chance to persuade the decision makers to go forward with the dive rescue. They cannot fail.

Master Sergeant Derek Anderson in base camp, pointing to a map of Tham Luang

25.
A Very Important Meeting

July 6, 2018

THAT NIGHT AT 10:00 P.M., every high-ranking Thai official at Tham Luang squeezes into the War Room, a tiny park headquarters building at the end of the parking lot. Minister of the Interior Paochinda is there, along with the rescue mission commander, Governor Narongsak. The commanders of the Navy SEALs and the Thai army are present, along with a host of other Thai military officers, officials, and academic advisers. Thanet and his father-in-law grab chairs at the back.

There is one man from the British camp in the meeting, but Rick, John, and Vern are all absent. They have already given their opinions multiple times and feel there is nothing more for them to add. Thanet wonders if it is for the best that the straight-talking Brits aren't here. Convincing so many Thai officials is going to be a delicate task. This calls for someone with the perfect mix of diplomacy and communication skills.

Luckily, the American officers seem to have that perfect mix. After official introductions, Major Charles Hodges begins his presentation.

The Tham Luang park building that became known as the War Room

He tells the room that from the moment his unit arrived at Tham Luang, they have refused to let their emotions sway their decision making. He knows how tense this moment is for the Thai leadership. Not only are they thinking about the children trapped in the cave; they are also thinking about the parents and loved ones waiting outside. They are thinking about the millions of people all over Thailand who are watching their every move with their hearts in their throats. Major Hodges knows how difficult it is for a Thai person to carry the burden of suggesting they go ahead with a plan that could end in death for some of the children. As a non-Thai, it's easier for him to make that recommendation.

Major Hodges goes on to describe the situation as it stands and tells the room how they have investigated every single option for trying to rescue the boys: alternative entrances, drilling, pumping the water, and even just leaving them inside until the dry season. Then he walks through all the problems with every one of those options.

He presents the only option they have left: diving the kids out. He acknowledges that the dive will be risky, but compared to any of the alternatives, it is really the safest course of action. He then turns the presentation over to Sergeant Derek Anderson, who goes through each step of the dive-rescue plan. True to his word, Sergeant Anderson presents a solid plan of attack. It's clear to everyone in the room that he has thought through all the details and gone over them multiple times. Sergeant Anderson leaves no doubt in anyone's mind that the dive rescues will be carefully carried out.

After the presentation, a group of Thai professors stand and speak up against the dive plan. "Why are we rushing?" they ask. "We should take our time, gather more data, analyze the numbers!"

Thanet, a man who loves data and trusts numbers, shakes his head. He knows that it doesn't matter how much more data they gather. They will never know for certain what the outcome will be. Time is running out. At this point, they're going to have to make a leap of faith.

Thanet then gives his report on the water-diversion team's efforts and explains how important controlling the water has been. Most of the people in the room had no idea what was happening with the water pumping at Sai Tong, or with the stream diversion on the mountainside, and they nod and murmur in surprise to learn of it.

With the formal presentations over, Governor Narongsak pulls Major Hodges aside and asks for his honest assessment: What is the likelihood of success?

As usual, Major Hodges doesn't sugarcoat the facts. He estimates a 60 to 70 percent success rate. Put more bluntly, he says, "I fully expect anywhere from three to five children to die."

Five out of thirteen.

They could lose almost half.

Major Hodges quickly adds that if they don't act now, his prediction of success will go down to zero. If they don't get the boys out of the cave soon, none of them will live.

THAM LUANG DIVE-RESCUE PLAN

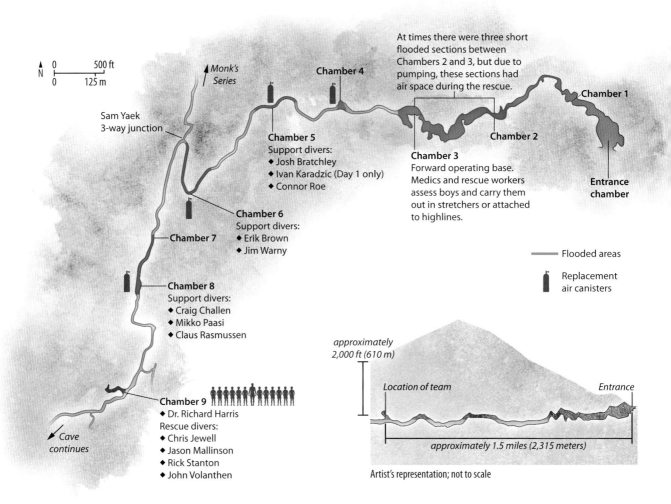

N
0   500 ft
0   125 m

Monk's Series

Chamber 4

At times there were three short flooded sections between Chambers 2 and 3, but due to pumping, these sections had air space during the rescue.

Chamber 1

Sam Yaek 3-way junction

Chamber 5
Support divers:
◆ Josh Bratchley
◆ Ivan Karadzic (Day 1 only)
◆ Connor Roe

Chamber 2

Chamber 3
Forward operating base. Medics and rescue workers assess boys and carry them out in stretchers or attached to highlines.

Entrance chamber

Chamber 6
Support divers:
◆ Erik Brown
◆ Jim Warny

Chamber 7

Flooded areas

Replacement air canisters

Chamber 8
Support divers:
◆ Craig Challen
◆ Mikko Paasi
◆ Claus Rasmussen

approximately 2,000 ft (610 m)

Location of team

Entrance

Chamber 9
◆ Dr. Richard Harris
Rescue divers:
◆ Chris Jewell
◆ Jason Mallinson
◆ Rick Stanton
◆ John Volanthen

Cave continues

approximately 1.5 miles (2,315 meters)

Artist's representation; not to scale

Minister Paochinda agrees. It's a tremendous responsibility to be the person who gives the go-ahead for a rescue that will likely end with casualties, but the minister is convinced that this is the only way forward, and he is ready to accept the risks. He orders that the plan be carried out swiftly.

As the War Room empties of people, Minister Paochinda asks Thanet and his father-in-law to sit with him. He explains to them that up until this point the prime minister has been in favor of the drilling option, and he will have the ultimate say. Minister Paochinda thinks the prime minister will support his decision, but he needs to send a letter to explain why diving is a better option than drilling.

Thanet blinks a few times, realizing that Minister Paochinda is asking *them* to help write this letter. He steadies his hand. And then Thanet, a no-rank, no-status Thai-American restaurant owner, picks up a pen and begins drafting a letter to the prime minister of Thailand.

With the ink dry, everything is in place.

They will have thirty-six hours to get ready.

Thanet Natisri and his father-in-law (left) seated with Minister Paochinda (right) after the conclusion of the big meeting

A Thai Navy SEAL prepares diving gear.

26.

Stage One: Rehearsals

July 7, 2018

A CAVE-DIVE RESCUE with this many people has never been attempted before.

A cave-dive rescue with children has never been attempted before.

Just a few weeks ago, the world's experts in cave-diving rescues would have deemed the whole thing impossible. At Tham Luang Nang Non, the rescue team is going to give the impossible a shot.

They have just a short time to get prepared. Any disagreements or misunderstandings that have bubbled up in base camp over the past two weeks must be set aside. The rescuers must now become a perfectly synchronized machine, with each person acting as a single gear. If even one person fails to do their job, the entire rescue machine will break down.

Planning the diving portion of the rescue is left almost entirely to Rick and John and their comrades. Fellow expert divers Chris Jewell and Jason Mallinson will join them in taking on the grave responsibility of diving the children out of the cave. They will be supported by a skilled team of cave divers from all over the world. Once the rescue begins, thirteen divers will be in place beyond Chamber 3: a small but highly trusted team.

From the moment that Rick and John begin thinking about diving the boys out of the cave, they decide that there are two requirements that must be met before they will agree to participate.

The first requirement is to find full-face masks that fit the children. On the day that John and Rick located the Wild Boars, one of the first things they noticed as the boys came down to the water to greet them was how small they were. Finding a mask that will form a good tight seal around their faces won't be easy. It can't be a typical mask that covers only the eyes and nose; the British divers want a mask that will cover the entire face so that the boys won't need to mess with holding a regulator in their mouths. Air will be constantly piped into the mask, keeping it at "positive pressure." This means that if the seal gets bumped or slightly loosened, air will bubble out instead of water rushing in and flooding the mask.

Finding the right mask turns out to be a huge challenge. The only masks that seem as though they will work are the kind used by industrial divers and firefighters. In the UK, a small dive shop named Bristol Channel Diving scours its supply and finally locates two of this type of mask. The precious items are rushed to the airport in London with a full police escort leading the way.

Ay and the Get-It-Done Crew call around to find a local child who can try on the masks and make sure they will fit. They find a young boy who gleefully volunteers to skip school to help. When he tries on one of the masks sent from England, it's still too big. It takes some makeshift last-minute engineering — including using cut-up pieces of neoprene from a wet suit — to finally get the masks to fit.

With this mask design, the Wild Boars can just inhale and exhale normally and won't have to think about their breathing at all. This is good because John and Rick's second requirement is that the boys be completely knocked out for the entire thing.

Knowing that panic is a diver's worst enemy, they have asked their friend Dr. Richard Harris to fly in from Adelaide, Australia, to join the dive team. In addition to being a top-tier cave diver, Dr. Harris is also a practicing anesthesiologist. His job back home is to give patients drugs that dull their pain and sedate them (put them to sleep) before they undergo surgery. It's a job that requires him to be incredibly levelheaded and cool under pressure. It's no surprise that those qualities also make him an excellent sump diver. He flies to northern Thailand with his long-time diving partner, veterinarian Craig Challen, another record-setting cave diver.

Dr. Harris's first thought on hearing the plan to sedate the Wild Boars is *No way*.

"Sedation is out of the question," he tells Rick. "It's impossible to do that safely and dive kids out in an anesthetized state."

He sedates children on a regular basis at his medical practice, where he has a reputation for being especially great with kids. But in those circumstances, the children are surrounded by other doctors and nurses. They have easy access to other drugs and medical equipment. It's much different from sedating kids in a dark, wet cave, far from emergency medical help if something goes wrong.

But once Dr. Harris arrives on-site and is fully briefed on the situation, he reluctantly agrees that having the boys sleep through the rescue is the safest way to get them out. With doubt weighing heavily on his mind, he begins calling other doctors to discuss which medicines to give the boys.

The boys' parents aren't told that their children will be sedated. In fact, this part of the mission isn't made public in Thailand at all while the rescue is taking place. Perhaps the Thai authorities worry how it sounds. The boys will be put to sleep and then dragged through the water? What if they never wake up? It sounds worrisome and dangerous to use sedation for something other than surgery. When the rescue begins, even some of the people working inside the cave will not be told that the boys are medicated.

The sedation and the diving will be the most dangerous part of the rescue for the boys because it puts them at immediate risk for drowning. But there is also a whole host of other things to plan for if the rescue is to be successful, such as figuring out how to get the boys over the dry sections of the cave. Major Hodges suggests they use one of his favorite problem-solving techniques. His air force team will huddle together and sketch out a plan. The Thai SEALs will design their own plan separately, and then the two teams will get together and compare. They will take the best ideas from each group to create the best possible plan.

With the details refined, the rescuers divide the route into nine separate chambers. At the start of each dive, Dr. Harris will give the Wild Boars their sedative in Chamber 9. The British divers — Rick, John, Chris, and Jason — will then dive the children through the sumps between Chambers 9 and 3. Along the way, support divers will be stationed in the dry sections to help swap out air tanks, give medical checks, and, if necessary, finish diving the boys out if the four other divers run into any problems. Everyone else, including the Thai SEALs and the US Air Force, will be waiting in Chamber 3 to finish taking the boys to the exit.

Once the overall plan is agreed upon, Sergeant Derek Anderson begins leading the rescue team in rehearsals. He clears a large area in the Tham Luang parking lot and stakes out a mini version of the cave, using plastic chairs to represent the chambers. He places water bottles on the ground to represent the air cylinders that will be staged at points along the route. He walks through the "cave," marking where they need more cylinders or rescue stretchers and how many people will need to carry them. Some in base camp eye him strangely, but this type of rehearsal is standard procedure for Sergeant Anderson and his squadron.

The rescue divers are rehearsing as well. They meet up at an indoor swimming pool with local children who have (again, gleefully) volunteered to miss school to help the rescue. The children try on the small wet suits, face masks, and gear, and the divers practice the best way to tow their small bodies underwater.

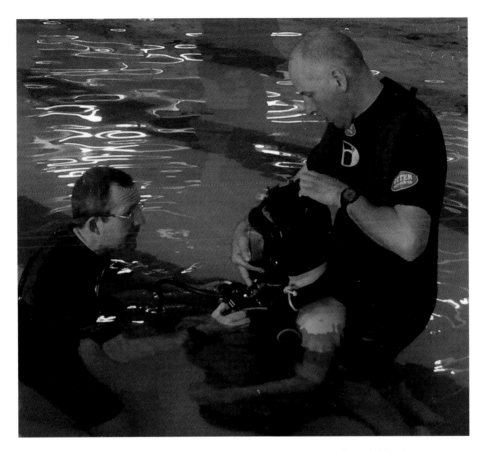

John Volanthen and Rick Stanton rehearse the dive rescue with a child volunteer at the local activity center swimming pool.

As the dive team makes its preparations, Colonel Singhanat and Thanet are strengthening their water-management efforts. As Governor Narongsak says in a press conference, "We are in a war against the water." All the pumping operations at Sai Tong must be maintained at full power. The diversion structures must be strengthened and repaired. If even one pump breaks down or one diversion structure fails, it could jeopardize the whole mission.

When Thanet is not with the water-diversion team on the mountain, he is bent over his laptop, poring through the data he has collected over the past week. He is looking for patterns in the rainfall.

Thanet knows that their water-control operations have been successful over the past few days in part because they haven't had much rain.

Practice Makes Perfect

Every astronaut, firefighter, pilot, and soldier will attest that rehearsing is a vital part of being successful in a crisis. We often hear incredible stories of pilots landing planes under emergency conditions or military units carrying out incredible feats of bravery under tremendous stress, and we marvel at the courage and quick reaction times of the heroes. What we hear less of is how much those heroes prepared both their bodies and their minds to be able to respond in those life-or-death situations.

The first time you entered your school building and had to find your classroom, you probably felt a little overwhelmed. You had to take in a lot of new information all at once and figure out what was important (which hall your classroom was in), and what was not (how many photos were stapled onto the bulletin board). By now you probably walk to class every day without even thinking about it. You can even talk with friends while you do it, and high-five your librarian along the way. Your body and your mind have practiced your route enough times that it's automatic.

The front section of your brain is dedicated to learning. When you are put into a strange situation, your brain's front section takes in new information, notices details, and decides which of those details are important and which ones don't matter. It creates a model and stores it in a different section of your brain. Any time you need to act fast, your brain pulls up that model from storage.

This is why flight attendants walk passengers through emergency procedures and why schools practice fire drills. It's why Sergeant Anderson has the rescuers pacing across a parking lot, pretending that plastic water bottles are scuba tanks. It's why Rick and John run through mental rehearsals before every dive.

Rehearsals put a plan of action into your body's muscle memory and into your brain's back compartments. That way you don't need to stop and think about what you're supposed to do. You can just do it.

He wants to figure out how much rainfall the cave can take on before the flooding inside overwhelms the pumps. After many calls to nearby weather stations and hours spent making graphs of the data, Thanet calculates that they can withstand 15 millimeters (a little over half an inch) of rain. Anything more than that, and the cave will start flooding again.

If this happens when the divers are already inside the cave, they could get trapped themselves. Rain is definitely in the forecast, but it's impossible to say how much. Thanet is a scientific person who likes to control every detail of a project as much as possible. But when it comes to the weather, the only thing he can do is hope.

Back at Tham Luang, SEALs clear the first three chambers of any unnecessary equipment. A green tarp is wrapped across the fence outside the entrance so that no one can see inside. The hundreds of journalists and camera crews are moved away from the cave, across the street, and the roads are cleared. Even though the rescue team has no idea if they will be bringing out living survivors or not, they order one ambulance for every child to wait on standby.

Low, heavy clouds begin to drift closer to the Nang Non mountains. Rescuers keep looking up nervously. They need the rain to hold off just a couple more days.

As night falls on July 7, the time for rehearsals is over. In the morning, the rescue will begin.

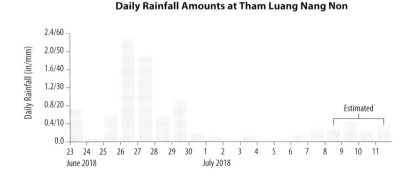

Daily Rainfall Amounts at Tham Luang Nang Non

Ambulances waiting on standby at Tham Luang

27.

Stage Two: "Today Is D-Day"

July 8, 2018

ON JULY 8 AT 10:00 A.M., the team of divers, SEALs, and military personnel file, stone-faced and serious, into Tham Luang. If everything goes smoothly, they expect it to take about five hours for the divers to access Chamber 9, prepare the children, and bring them back to the forward base in Chamber 3.

Everyone wishes they could bring the entire team out at once. But there aren't enough masks, capable rescue divers, or hours in a day to get it all done. They have acquired four full-face masks, which means they can bring four boys out today. But who will be first?

Dr. Harris has told the Thai SEALs that all the boys are both physically and mentally fit enough for the journey, so it doesn't matter in what order the children are dived out. The decision has been left up to the Wild Boars themselves. Coach Ek huddled the team together the day before to discuss the order of the rescue. No one was particularly keen to be first. All the boys have bonded with the SEALs and with Dr. Pak. All of a sudden it seemed hard to leave them, and hard to leave the group. Coach Ek suggested that the boys who live farthest away from the cave should be the ones to exit first. That way they can go through town and tell everyone along the way that the rest of the team is coming out. The Wild Boars have no idea that not only are their parents anxiously waiting just outside, but the entire world is watching to see if they are going to make it.

Using this logic, Note, Tern, Night, and Nick will go first. The second group will be Dom, Adul, Bew, and Mix. Finally, Titan, Thi, Pong, and Mark will be brought out on the third day, along with Coach Ek. Dr. Pak and the three Thai SEALs will dive themselves through after all the boys are out.

The boys have been prepared for the process. The day before, Dr. Harris and his dive partner, Craig Challen, dived all the way back to Chamber 9 to get comfortable with the conditions. Dr. Harris had a note for the boys, translated into Thai:

1. You will take a tablet that will make you feel funny.
2. Come down to the waterside and sit with me.
   Get a shot in one leg.
   Get a shot in the other leg.
3. Fall asleep.
4. Wake up in bed.

Dr. Harris watched the boys' faces for signs of fear. Instead, the boys nodded. To him, they seemed sort of unemotional about the whole thing. *Yup. Yeah. Yup.* Not a trace of panic on anyone's face.

Dr. Harris had been impressed and relieved that the boys seemed so at ease with the terrifying journey they were about to take. It's hard to imagine that out of all twelve kids, not one of them was nervous about getting shots or being dived out of the cave. But the children were likely being both polite and practical. It would've been bad behavior to make a fuss about it. Plus, it didn't matter whether they made a fuss or not; this was the only way they were getting out of the cave, so they might as well cooperate. They trusted the men taking care of them, and they focused on that last step in the process: finally waking up in a bed, outside the cave.

Even though the boys seem very cool about the plan, Dr. Harris asks the SEALs to take the group up the hill and around the corner so they don't have to see their friends getting the injection. No matter how brave you are, it's no fun watching other people get shots.

Fourteen-year-old Note is up first. He is kitted up in multiple wet suits to keep him warm, a buoyancy vest, and a hood. He takes antianxiety medicine, and then he is injected with the sedative.

Once all the drugs are given, Dr. Harris fits Note with the precious full-face mask that has been flown halfway around the globe just for this mission. Note's wrists and ankles are secured with zip ties to protect his arms and legs from dragging and getting injured. The valve on Note's air tank is opened, and his mask fills with air that is 80 percent oxygen. Breathing this mixture will help ensure that Note's blood absorbs the maximum amount of oxygen. That extra oxygen will buy his brain cells precious time if his mask floods or if he has problems breathing along the way.

Dr. Harris would like to hope for zero problems, but he knows that isn't likely. With Note fully sedated and fitted with his mask, the doctor gently lowers the boy's face under the water to check the seal. It's a bizarre moment, dipping a kid's face underwater in the back of a pitch-black cave, but nothing about this mission has been ordinary. Note's breathing halts for a moment. Dr. Harris counts. After about thirty seconds, he sees the bubbles streaming from the outlet valve of Note's mask. He's breathing normally. It's time to go.

Jason Mallinson has volunteered to be the first rescue diver. He checks his own gear, and then Note's one last time. Then he slides the boy off the slope and pulls him underwater. Dr. Harris watches the light from Jason's headlamp glow hazily under the surface, and then they are gone.

Fall Asleep, Wake Up in Bed

After many conversations with coworkers, Dr. Harris has finally decided to give the boys a sedative called ketamine. Ketamine is a common drug used during surgeries when the patient needs to be unconscious, such as having their wisdom teeth removed. Given the right amount, the patient will go to sleep and stay asleep even if they are getting a tooth yanked out of their skull. Unless the patient is already really sick to begin with, it's difficult to overdose, or take too much of the drug. Because of this, ketamine is commonly used in "field" situations, like for soldiers on a battlefield or in natural disasters. Still, figuring out the right amount to give the kids has been agonizing for Dr. Harris.

Because children have a higher metabolism than adults, their bodies process drugs in their bloodstream faster. That means they wear off faster, too. Dr. Harris is worried about the drugs wearing off before the boys are out of the cave. One side effect of ketamine is that patients can have intense hallucinations as the drugs wear off. Dr. Harris imagines what would happen if a boy came out of his sleep confused and hallucinating while underwater. How could he not panic? It would be a disaster.

But Dr. Harris is also wary of giving the boys too much of the sedative. It's hard to say how the Wild Boars' bodies have been affected by their time in the cave and how they will respond to the drugs. Large doses of ketamine can cause apnea, or short periods where one doesn't breathe. The apnea is temporary, and once the boys' breathing resumed, the ketamine would actually stimulate their lungs to breathe. But it's something to worry about. If the children have any problems when they are in the middle of a sump, there will be no way for their rescue diver to help them. A boy could die, and his diver wouldn't be able to do anything except drag his body to the exit.

In the end, Dr. Harris decides that the biggest danger is the boys waking up and panicking underwater. In that case, both the child and his rescue diver would certainly die. He has decided to go with a dose of 5 milligrams of ketamine per kilogram of the child's weight — a pretty big dose. Even then, he expects the drug will wear off after about forty minutes, so he gives each rescue diver additional syringes to give the boys top-up doses along the way.

Before they take the ketamine, the boys will be given a tablet of a drug called alprazolam, which is an antianxiety medicine. It reduces the likelihood that they will panic about what's to come: receiving the injection, putting on the face mask, and sliding into the cold water. It will also help reduce the hallucinations. The tablet usually causes people to have amnesia, or forget what happens to them, so not only will the Wild Boars be asleep for their extraction, they hopefully won't remember any of it.

The ketamine will be injected straight into the leg muscle, which will help it release into the bloodstream more steadily than if it's injected under the skin. In one leg: the ketamine sedative. In the other leg: atropine. Another side effect of the ketamine is that it increases your body's secretions. Patients on ketamine cough and drool, and tears leak out of their eyes. The atropine helps dry all this up. That's very important because the last thing anyone wants is for the boys to start choking or coughing on their own saliva while they are underwater.

Divers Erik Brown and Mikko Paasi staging tanks and maintaining guidelines

28.
Alone in the Dark

July 8, 2018

JASON MALLINSON IS DIVING with Note through the long, flooded passage between Chambers 9 and 8. It's slow, tough going. At one point the passage squeezes down to the diameter of a garbage can. One of Jason's hands holds the guideline. The other grips tight to a strap on the back of Note's buoyancy vest. A short tether clipped to each of their bodies connects the two and will keep them from getting separated in a crisis. Jason cradles Note close to his own body. His number one worry at this point is that Note's face mask will somehow get dislodged.

The thin seal around the mask is the only thing standing between life and death for Note. If he sees the mask flooding, Jason will have to swim as fast as possible and give Note CPR before his brain cells become starved of oxygen. As harrowing as that would be, it's better than the alternative, which is that Note's mask leaks and the boy begins to drown without Jason realizing it.

Underwater, the passages are peppered with boulders and stalagmites, none of which Jason can see through the murky swill. He holds

Note tight to his chest, keeping the boy's head near his own face. Rather than risk knocking him against a rock or the cave wall, Jason takes all the knocks with his own helmet. With the boy's head so close to his own, Jason can feel the stream of bubbles coming from the mask. That's exactly the sign that he needs right now.

It should take twenty minutes to dive through the first sump. Later, Jason will say, "I was confident of being able to take one of those kids and dive them out. I was not fully confident of getting them out alive."

Danish diving instructor Claus Rasmussen is one of eight international support divers stationed at dry points along the route. These men have been at Tham Luang since July 2, doing the grueling, dangerous work of staging air tanks along the dive route—the same task that Saman Gunan died doing. Claus has lived in southern Thailand for fifteen years with his Thai wife and their children, including a son who is about the same age as the boys they will attempt to rescue today.

Together with cave divers Craig Challen and Mikko Paasi, Claus will help carry the boys across Chamber 8 in a stretcher, replenish their air supply if needed, perform a medical check, and dive the boys out himself if for some reason the other rescue divers can't continue.

Claus, Mikko, and Craig are waiting for Jason. And waiting. Has he run into a problem?

Finally, they hear his voice call out behind them, asking what the heck they are doing standing there (but with much stronger language). The crew realize they've been waiting in the wrong place! The cave is so confusing inside, and the divers had misunderstood where they were supposed to stand. An already exhausted Jason has had to lug Note over dry land after diving him through a sump the length of three soccer fields.

Once they make sure that Jason and Note are safely on their way into the next sump, Claus's team hurries back to the water at the edge of Chamber 8. They arrive in time to see the headlamp of the second rescue

Mikko Paasi preparing the sked for the first child to come out

diver glowing beneath the water. But it's the strong stream of bubbles rippling the surface that brings Claus the most relief. This rescue diver is using a rebreather, which doesn't emit bubbles, so the bubbles Claus sees mean that the boy is breathing.

The support divers gently place the boy onto a rescue stretcher called a sked and carry him through Chamber 8. They slog through tacky mud, stumble over rocks, and wade through chest-high water. They don't want to slip, but they also need to hurry. Anesthesia causes a patient's core temperature to drop, so one of the biggest dangers to the boys is hypothermia. They need to get each child out of the cave as quickly as possible so that they can warm up and revive safely.

Claus's crew delivers this second boy, then a third safely across the chamber. Some relief starts to set in that things are going well so far.

Mikko Paasi and Claus Rasmussen in Chamber 3 preparing to dive

But when they get back to the water's edge with the sked for the fourth child, they find Rick Stanton and Dr. Harris kneeling beside Night. Rick is Night's rescue diver. Since Night is the last rescue of the day, Dr. Harris has followed up behind them for support. And it's a good thing that he did.

Night is in trouble.

Dr. Harris lies down on the sand with the boy, spooning his body for warmth. Night is breathing too faintly, holding his breath too long before taking another. The boy has been battling mild pneumonia, and this is the textbook reaction of a child with a chest infection on ketamine. The problem is that they aren't in a hospital or a clinic, where there would be equipment and medications to help; they are in a cave, lying on the dirt. All Dr. Harris can do is hold Night's mouth open and make sure that he has a clear airway to his lungs.

Time crawls for an agonizingly long thirty minutes. Claus thinks about Major Hodges's grim statistics and wonders if this will be the first life they are going to lose. Finally, Night recovers and resumes taking normal breaths. They get him onto the stretcher and make sure that his breathing is regular before carrying him through to the next sump.

Claus and his friends watch Rick swim away with Night. They have done their part. Now they will have to dive out themselves before they can find out whether any of the boys they saw today made it out of the cave alive.

The waiting is the hardest part.

Jason Mallinson is nearly wiped out. He has dived through two long sumps already and staggered over dry land carrying Note's limp body. This is all in addition to hiking into the cave in the morning and diving for hours just to get to the boys.

One of the trickiest parts of the journey is a sump that curls upward until it's nearly vertical. Even though Jason has dived this section before, it's impossible for him to remember where the vertical section is until his head rams into the wall. The passage is too narrow for Note and him to fit through together at the same time. He tries pushing the boy ahead of him. Note's body tends to float horizontally, and Jason must be careful not to force off his mask. When that doesn't work, he tries going in first and pulling the boy behind. That doesn't work either. It takes several minutes just to figure out how to tackle this one section.

Jason gets through and is now swimming along a section of the cave that is only partially flooded, with air to breathe at the top. Pulling an unconscious boy along at the surface is even harder than diving with him underwater, where he is practically weightless.

Jason is neck-deep in water when Note begins to stir out of his unconscious state. It must be time to give him his top-up dose of sedative. Dr. Harris has told the rescue divers that if they're unsure about the dose, they should give the child a bigger injection of sedative rather than a smaller one. The worst disaster would be if the children wake up.

Jason pulls the injection kit out of his dry suit. It's awkward trying to float at the surface, hold on to a floppy body, and put together a needle all at the same time. Extra syringes float in the water around him. He holds on to Note with one hand, fumbling to put the needle and syringe together with the other. Aside from practicing on a plastic water bottle the day before, he has never given a shot in his life, and now he'll have to give it to a child, floating in the water, in the middle of a cave, without a soul in the world to help him. He manages to get the boy's leg up to the surface, jab in the needle, and give him the proper dose. Note slips back into unconsciousness.

After gathering up the floating supplies and stuffing them back into his dry suit, Jason gets ready to submerge again. As frightening as this moment has been, he will have to perform three more injections along the way. He still has a long way to go.

Master Sergeant Derek Anderson of the US Air Force 320th Special Tactics Squadron is at his post at the edge of Chamber 3. He has his cell phone ready to text his commanding officer, Major Charles Hodges, as soon as there is any sign of one of the rescue divers. Sergeant Anderson checks the time once again before returning to his current fixation: watching a rope.

The rope is the guideline that extends down into the dark water between Chambers 3 and 4. Sergeant Anderson knows that even before he sees the first diver's headlamp, he will see that rope twitch.

It has been a little over five hours since the rescue divers set off from Chamber 3 at the start of the day. Any moment now, they should be surfacing. That is, unless there have been problems.

Sergeant Anderson checks behind him to make sure that everything is in place for the rest of the extraction. More than one hundred rescuers are staged between Chamber 3 and the cave mouth, waiting to ferry the boys safely to the exit, where ambulances are ready to zip them to a helicopter that will take them to the hospital in Chiang Rai.

Other than the rescue divers and a few other key members of the rescue team, no one knows the order in which the boys will be brought out. Most of the rescuers standing by have no idea whom they are waiting for. They only know that it will be a miracle if the boy who emerges from the water is still alive.

Vern Unsworth stands at his station with all the others. He has supported this dive rescue from the beginning. What if today goes horribly wrong? There is nothing he can do now but wait to see if the cave that is like a second home to him will finally release the boys it has held captive for more than two weeks.

Time clicks by slowly. Every rescuer checks and rechecks their gear.

And then suddenly everyone's attention is on the water at the edge of Chamber 3.

The rope is twitching.

Rescuers carrying a sked through the entrance chamber

29.
Mission Possible

July 8, 2018

JASON MALLINSON climbs out of the water at Chamber 3 and carefully hands off Note to the waiting crew. The boy is loaded onto the last rescue sked of the journey, and his diving mask is removed.

When some of the Thai rescuers see him, they fear the worst. Not everyone has been told that the Wild Boars would be sedated, so they thought the boys would walk out of the water on their own. Watching the limp body laid onto the stretcher fills them with dread. Surely something is wrong.

Medics check Note's pulse.

He's alive.

They quickly measure his other vital signs: his body temperature, the percentage of oxygen in his blood, and his breathing rate. He is only barely conscious, weakly moving his hands as he lies on the stretcher.

The rescuers are relieved, but they know they are not out of the woods yet.

* * *

HOW THE RESCUERS GOT THE BOYS OUT

Chamber 3
The boys are transferred to stretchers for the rest of their journey out of the cave.

Chamber 2
The rescue team guides stretchers along two zip lines over the jagged cave floor below.

Chamber 1
The rescuers navigate steps and rough terrain to reach the cave's exit.

Exit

Approximately 1/2 mile (600 meters)

Chambers 9–4
The boys are dived and carried through approximately one mile (1600 meters) of cave passage.

Chamber 2
The stretchers are placed on rafts that the rescuers push across the partially flooded chamber.

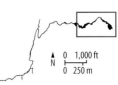

N 0   1,000 ft
   0 250 m

*Artist's representation; not to scale

The remaining 2,600 feet (800 meters) of Tham Luang is full of steep, slippery climbs through passages that are still partially full of water, so handling the boy safely is no easy matter. In some places, Note is literally passed from hand to hand, like a package traveling over a human conveyor belt. Each rescuer watches the boy's face as he passes by, checking for signs of trouble. On one steep downward section, the rescue team has laid flattened pump hoses side by side on the ground. It looks a bit like a bounce-house slide. Note's sked is placed on top and gently slides down the slope, with rescuers keeping hold of him the entire way. If Note were conscious and his life weren't at stake, this would be the fun part.

In two places the ground is perilously steep, so zip lines made of rope and pulleys have been secured to the rocks. Note's sked is clipped in with carabiners and lifted high above the rocky slopes.

Vern is stationed at the second zip line, operating the ropes with other rescue personnel. He focuses on his task, steadily pulling the line, hand over hand. Note sails silently over the heads of rescuers. And then he is carried out of Vern's sight, to the entrance. After sixteen days, Tham Luang has let the first Wild Boar go free.

Thanet Natisri is with his team on the slopes above Pha Mee Village, reinforcing their diversion structures, when he feels the buzz of his cell phone. The message is from Sergeant Derek Anderson.

The first boy is out of the cave. Alive.

He shouts the news to his team. Some of them burst into tears. They can't help it. They have been working so hard, pushing their bodies to the very limit, for days. Their only hope was that all their work would make a difference. It has.

Down the mountain at Sai Tong cave, Colonel Singhanat's phone chimes. He has no information about which boy has come out. He only knows that the child's status is green: alive and stable.

He waves his arms at the water-pumping crew. When the farmers and soldiers hear the message, they lift their arms to the sky and cheer so loudly that they momentarily drown out the thrum of the super-pumps.

In base camp, Governor Narongsak gets the text message about the first boy. A few minutes later, the second boy is brought out, also alive. A third. And then even Night, who had so much trouble breathing, has made it out safely. This is such a relief. This is the outcome everyone was afraid to even wish for. Soon, the governor will relay the news to the waiting media.

But first, he will go to tell the most important people on the mountain.

The boys' parents cheer! And then they each break down and cry.

There is a flurry of calls and texts to grandmothers and aunties, uncles and cousins and neighbors, who also cheer and then break down and cry. Cheers and cries follow the boys as the ambulances zip them down the Tham Luang park road to the waiting helicopter. When their

Thanet Natisri and members of the water-diversion team cheering

classmates, who have been glued to the news coverage on television, hear the announcement, they jump in the air and shout with joy. Soon the cheering and crying spreads down the mountain to Mae Sai, across the province. It spreads across the entire country of Thailand.

In small towns, neighbors rush out from their houses and embrace one another. In the buzzing capital of Bangkok, strangers erupt into cheers on the Skytrain. Bursts of applause fill restaurants and bars, whose televisions have been playing nonstop coverage of Tham Luang for weeks.

People watch the moment again and again on their cell phones, a smiling Governor Narongsak speaking into the glare of photographers' lights: "After sixteen days, we finally get to see the Wild Boars in the flesh."

The news is beamed to satellites floating above the globe and then down again to people all over the world who have been anxiously waiting. Across oceans and time zones, people who have never even been to Thailand pump their fists in the air. On the other side of the planet, people wake up hours before dawn to check the news on their phones. They smile and then turn to their sleeping family members and whisper tearfully, "They did it. They got the first four out."

Rain over the Nang Non mountains

30.
The Sleeping Lady Has the Final Say

July 9–10, 2018

FOUR MEMBERS OF THE WILD BOARS are now resting in the Prachanukroh Hospital in Chiang Rai.

The boys' parents are elated. The entire world is ecstatic. And the rescue team is encouraged that all their planning and grueling work is paying off.

But they also know that this is no time to relax, either physically or mentally.

They have brought four people out safely, but they still have nine members of the soccer team, plus three Thai SEALs and Dr. Pak, inside.

Luckily, the second day of the rescue goes even more smoothly than the day before. Adul, Nick, Dom, and Bew are brought out, one by one, two hours quicker than the group the previous day. The rescue divers are getting more comfortable with carrying the sedated boys with them. They have figured out when they need to turn the boys a particular way, or when to tuck them under an arm to get through the tightest squeezes without having to take off any gear. Even though the divers tried to be

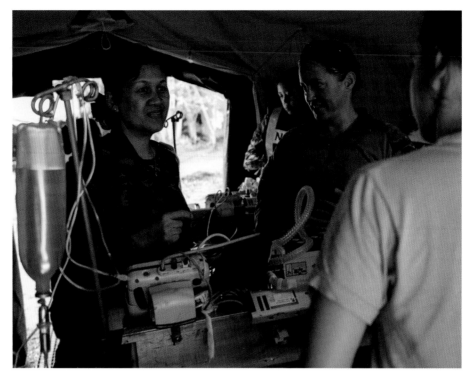

Thai and US military medics are on-site to provide support once the boys are brought through the cave.

gentle, the first four Wild Boars took quite a few knocks and scrapes to the head on their way out. For the remaining rescues, they pad the boys' wet suit hoods with extra neoprene to cushion them.

People lining the roadside cheer as four more ambulances rush by with four more boys inside. The rescuers are exhausted. It's been another long, full day of diving and hiking with heavy gear on their backs. The divers' hands are shredded and infected. They haven't been able to wear gloves because that would prevent them from feeling the precious guideline. They had wanted to take a day of rest in between each day of the operation, but everyone realizes that they have to beat the rain. They will just have to hold on to their focus and muster their energy for one final push.

* * *

Thanet's team has not eased up on their grueling schedule for a moment. The rescue divers have reported that when they swam into Sam Yaek junction, they didn't feel the same gush of warm, clear water coming in from the right-hand side. That means that Thanet's diversion structures have been working to keep the water from getting into Monk's Series. They just have to keep it up for one more day.

On the night of July 9, Thanet opens the door to his hotel room and kicks off his rain boots. Like most people who have been working at Tham Luang, his feet are wrecked. The constant wetness has led to a foot fungus, and his skin is peeling off in chunks. He'll have to go to a doctor as soon as this is all finished. He collapses on the bed, exhausted.

At 4:00 a.m., Thanet wakes to a horrifying sound: rain pelting the roof.

He rushes to the window and sees rain pouring down in sheets. This is not good. It rained on the first two days of the rescue, but only in scattered bursts that didn't last long. Sergeant Derek Anderson has asked Thanet to update him regularly on the rainfall. He doesn't want to send in the rescue divers if they know a big storm will blow in and trap the team inside. Thanet watches the rain, wondering if it's enough to put them over the 15-millimeter limit that will cause the cave to start flooding. He urgently hopes that the storm will blow over.

It doesn't. At 6:00 a.m., it's still raining hard. Thanet wonders if it's heavy enough to flood the cave and stop the rescue. He thinks of the nine people still trapped inside. Will the divers be able to get them out?

His phone starts pinging with messages. Derek Anderson wants to know what's up with the rain. The British divers want to know what's up with the rain. Thanet calls each weather station and scrawls notes on a pad. They are up to 14 millimeters of rain in the area above Monk's Series — a paper clip's width away from the limit. He calls his teammates, who are checking out the diversion structures. They tell him that so far everything is holding up.

A US Air Force service member demonstrates the highline technique used to carry the boys out through Chamber 2.

Thanet calls Sergeant Derek Anderson and gives him the report. The sergeant tells Thanet to keep him updated. The divers are going inside.

Vern Unsworth stands at his regular post, manning the ropes at one of the highlines near the entrance. He is listening. "Do you hear that?" he asks one of the other volunteers.

"No. Hear what?"

Vern realizes that only his highly trained ear can detect the change. He can hear the sound of moving water, far back in the cave. Tham Luang is starting to fill. He thinks about Major Hodges's bleak estimate that they would lose up to five of the boys during this rescue. They haven't lost anyone yet. He hopes they don't start now.

Today, the rescue divers have to bring out five Wild Boars instead of just four: Titan, Mark, and Pong, who are the smallest boys; Thi, the

group timekeeper and Coach Ek's right-hand man; and Coach Ek himself. The plan is that Jason Mallinson, Chris Jewell, Rick Stanton, and John Volanthen will take the first four out. But instead of continuing on after the first sump, Jason will hand his human cargo off to Irish support diver Jim Warny, who will continue the rest of the dive. Jason will then go back to Chamber 9, get the very last Wild Boar, and dive him all the way out of the cave.

Coach Ek is first up for the rescue today. The rescuers had considered not sedating him at all, but after the first day goes well, Coach asks to be given the same treatment as the boys. Jason Mallinson carries the sleeping coach through the first sump, hands him off to Jim Warny, and then returns through the sump to Chamber 9.

One by one, Rick, John, and Chris carry out their boys, leaving Jason to come last with Mark. When it's Mark's turn to be fitted into his wet suit and gear, Jason Mallinson discovers a problem. A huge one.

The boy's face mask doesn't fit.

Because there are five people to rescue today, they needed to have one extra full-face mask. The fifth face mask was flown in just yesterday. It's similar to the others, so it should fit, but they haven't had time to test it. As Jason holds it up to Mark's face, it's clear that it's too big to form a proper seal. Jason straps the mask on and cinches it as tight as possible, but there is still a gap under Mark's chin. Without an airtight seal, water will leak in and Mark could drown.

Jason has a critical decision to make. Is there time to go out, get a smaller mask, and come back for Mark? He doesn't think so. On his way into Chamber 9, Jason could definitely tell that the current is stronger than the previous two days. The water is rising inside Tham Luang, and there is no way to know how fast that rise will happen. If Mark is getting out at all, he has to come out now. Jason decides to improvise.

Cave divers always carry an extra mask with them. Jason has one spare full-face mask that isn't as robust as the others, but maybe it will work. With Mark now unconscious, Jason places it on the boy's face.

Miraculously, he is able to get the mask to seal. The seal isn't nearly as strong as the other masks, but that is all he has.

Jason pulls the sleeping Mark into the water with him, and the two of them are off on the last dive rescue of the mission.

Closer to the entrance, rescue diver Chris Jewell has also run into trouble. He is in the homestretch, between Chambers 4 and 3, holding Pong under one arm. Chris is so tired. The current today is stronger than the previous two days, which should make the dive out faster, since the divers will be swimming with the flow. But the water doesn't flow like a gentle, meandering river. It eddies and swirls, stirring up silt in the passages, making it extremely disorienting.

Chris lets go of the guideline for just a few seconds so that he can change his grip on the boy under his arm. In those brief seconds, he loses the line completely.

It's a diver's worst nightmare: being lost in a cave.

He reaches, feeling for the rope with his fingers, but he doesn't find it. Chris sweeps his arm out ahead of him, grasping at the water. His hand touches a line, but it isn't the guideline. It's an electrical cable that must have been installed a week ago, before this part of the cave flooded.

If Chris were alone, he would be able to take his time, get his bearings, and search for the proper line. He has plenty of oxygen left in his cylinders. But he isn't worried about himself; he's worried about the boy tucked under his arm. They've been diving for hours now, and he needs to get Pong out of the water before he wakes up out of his sedation or gets hypothermia.

Chris reasons that the electrical cable must lead out of the cave. He holds on to it and begins kicking.

When you are swimming in a fully enclosed space, with no signals to tell you which direction to go, it's alarmingly easy to lose your way. Your ear canals fill with water, messing with your internal compass. Unless the

water is clear and the current is smooth, you can think you're swimming in one direction while you are heading the opposite way entirely.

This is exactly what happens to Chris.

The mistake is easy to make, and it is one that can kill a cave diver. But luckily for Chris and Pong, they reach the surface. Chris looks around, thinking he should be in Chamber 3 by now. But where is everyone? He climbs up onto a dry spot and pulls Pong out of the water. After finding a discarded thermal blanket nearby, he wraps it around Pong to keep him warm, then takes off his fins and walks ahead, searching for a sign of where he is. It takes him a few minutes to realize he has swum deeper into the cave, back to Chamber 4.

Chris hears a voice in the dark chamber. It's Dr. Harris, who is on his way out. Chris explains what happened, and Dr. Harris offers to take Pong the rest of the way out to Chamber 3 so the exhausted Chris can follow behind.

The three of them arrive at their destination in Chamber 3 just behind Jason Mallinson, who passed them while they were getting their bearings in Chamber 4. Jason has managed to dive Mark out safely. To protect the delicate seal around Mark's face mask, Jason kept the boy's head tight under his chin, even though it meant that Jason had to take dozens of knocks to his own skull. His technique worked, and the flimsy seal on Mark's mask held long enough to get him to the finish line.

At 6:47 p.m., after eighteen days of being trapped underground, the last child is loaded onto the last ambulance and taken to the hospital. Every Wild Boar has been carried out of Tham Luang, alive and well.

But the rescue still isn't complete. The three Thai Navy SEALs and Dr. Pak are still on their way out. The Thai SEALs and the US Air Force are brothers-in-arms, and Major Charles Hodges instructs his troops: "Our mission is not done until every person is out of that cave."

The four remaining men have to space themselves out during their exit dive. The mud and silt swirling inside Tham Luang is so intense that divers have been emerging from the water with regulators full of dirt. Without a working regulator, there is no way for a diver to breathe the precious air in their tank. To prevent the divers from stirring up silt that could be a problem for those behind them, the four Thais dive out at forty-five-minute intervals.

The first Thai diver comes up in Chamber 3. Forty-five minutes later, up pops the second. Everything is happening on time so far. But as the third Thai diver emerges, workers in Chamber 3 hear a disturbing, loud bang. They look down and see the water rising.

Major Hodges gets a text from Chamber 3 that one of the pumps has failed. They need to evacuate. Right now. The chamber is beginning to flood, and they still haven't seen the last Thai SEAL yet. Workers begin grabbing whatever equipment they can carry. They leave everything else behind as water pools at their ankles, then creeps higher and higher. The levels are rising fast. Will they have to leave one last man inside?

Later, Major Hodges will describe the moment as something "like a movie": the last SEAL finally breaks the surface, and everyone scrambles to get out of Chamber 3 as the water surges up behind them.

It seems that the Sleeping Lady has had quite enough. As the last person steps out of the cave, the passages fill with water. They will remain filled for months.

The rescuers emerge from the cave mouth to thunderous applause and the flash of a thousand cameras. The relief is enormous. They carried the worries of the world when they carried the boys through the cave, and somehow they succeeded.

Major Charles Hodges has avoided interacting with the boys' families, but now they ask to speak with him. They bow to him and give him warm and tearful thanks. The air force commander who has insisted on keeping emotion at bay finally lets up on his number one rule.

He's not the only one. Finally, soaking wet, caked in mud, with blistered feet and sliced-up hands, the rescuers who have kept a laser focus on their mission allows themselves to smile and hug each other. It's over.

It's finally over. As they join in the cheers and high fives, the strange reality of the moment starts to sink in.

Somehow, they have defied the terrible odds. This rescue was impossible, and they did it anyway. They got them out alive—all thirteen.

Support divers Erik Brown and Mikko Paasi exit Tham Luang after the mission is completed

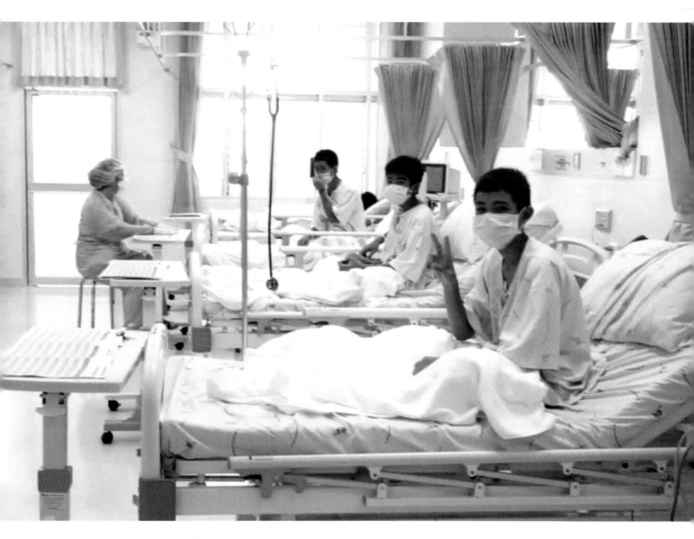

The Wild Boars recovering in a hospital in Chiang Rai

31.
It Should Not Have Worked

WHEN THE BOYS WAKE UP in the hospital, groggy and weak, they see their parents standing behind a window, waving tearfully. The doctors have chosen to keep the boys isolated to protect their immune systems. At the sight of their families, the boys cry. They are indescribably relieved and happy. Their parents feel the same. Finally, finally, the parents get to see the sons they had come so close to losing forever.

Soon, they get to cross the barrier and put their arms around their children, cradle their faces, and cry all over again. Their sons are so much thinner than the last time they held them, but incredibly, all thirteen Wild Boars are in good health. This is despite the many knocks to the head and dips in body temperature they experienced during their extraction. Coach Ek's core temperature right after his rescue was measured at 84°F (29°C) — a full 11 degrees Fahrenheit below the threshold for hypothermia. Thi woke up from his sedation with a fever, and Night and several others have had to take antibiotics for chest infections, but that's about it. None of the boys remember anything about the rescue.

After a few days, the boys record video messages thanking everyone who helped with the rescue or prayed for their return. They smile behind their paper face masks as they talk about the first non-hospital foods they'll eat when they get home: crispy pork, rice, Japanese sushi. Adul puts in a request for Kentucky Fried Chicken. Four of the boys passed their birthdays inside the cave: Night, Nick, Note, and Dom. There were no celebrations at the time, and their families intend to make up for it.

While they are still resting up in the hospital, the doctors wheel in a television so they can watch the final match of the World Cup. The boys' favorite team, England, has sadly been knocked out, so they cheer for France instead. Little Mark shouts the loudest of everyone—except for the doctors. This is the World Cup, after all.

After a week of recuperation, the kids are finally given the OK to go home. They bid a tearful and grateful goodbye to the doctors and nurses who took such good care of them. The hospital staff gives them some advice: Go back to your normal life as much as you can. Be with people who love you and who will make you feel safe. The boys go home with their families to sleep in their own beds. Coach Ek returns to the place in Mae Sai he calls home: the temple, Wat Doi Wao.

The rest of the team will soon join him. No one told the Wild Boars much about the rescue until they were safely recovering in the hospital. Gently, doctors broke the news to them about Saman Gunan's death. Everyone cried. All the boys felt a heavy weight of sadness. They thought about the Navy SEALs and Dr. Pak, who had cared for them in Chamber 9 and who had come to feel like family. Saman had sacrificed his own life to save theirs. He was also family, though they would never meet him.

The team agrees that they want to honor Saman's memory. They want to do something to show their deep gratitude for everyone who worked so hard to get them out of Tham Luang. They decide that all the Buddhist boys will become novice monks at Wat Doi Wao. This temple is a familiar place for them, where they go every day after school to play and hang out (and eat leftover food that the monks don't finish). The boys are willing to serve out a full term of three months, but the senior monk wants them to return to school and their normal lives. It is decided that the boys will be monks for nine days, the same number of nights they were trapped inside Chamber 9 before they were found.

With Coach Ek, the boys go through the ordination ceremony. Their heads are shaved and washed, and they are blessed. They dress in the saffron-colored robes (and probably have to help one another into them!) and take the novice monk's oath. Now they get a deep teaching of the prayer and meditation that kept up their will to survive inside the cave. These practices will strengthen the boys from the inside out, building a solid foundation that will keep them steady after they leave the temple.

On August 6, the boys return to school and arrive to a joyous welcome from their classmates. It is so good to be back! Their friends have been waiting eagerly for this day. Now they'll get to joke with their buddies

The Wild Boars in the hospital showing the messages of gratitude they wrote on a portrait of Saman Gunan

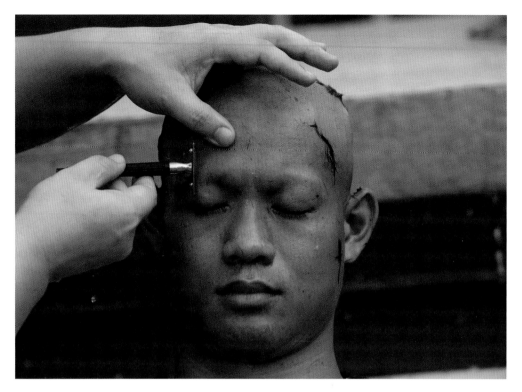

Coach Ek's head being shaved as part of the ordination ceremony at Wat Doi Wao

again, and things will start to feel like normal. The Wild Boars' classmates all promise to help the boys catch up on their studies and tutor them in the lessons they missed. Plans are hatched to go out to eat as soon as possible.

On August 8, Coach Ek and the three boys who were stateless are all granted Thai citizenship. They can now travel outside the country, study, and work without fear of punishment. There are still up to 3.5 million stateless people living in the shadows in Thailand, including hundreds of thousands of refugees, many of whom are children. The rescue of the Wild Boars has drawn more attention to this problem and has increased calls by activists to address it. There is hope that the Wild Boars' rescue and political changes in Thailand will lead to reforms that will bring stateless people in Thailand out of the shadows and into the light.

The Wild Boars after their novice monk ordination ceremony at Wat Doi Wao

Now that the Wild Boars are home, their lives are both back to normal and forever changed. The boys who once imagined having to bike home alone after getting out of the cave have become international celebrities. Strangers stop them on the street to take photos with them. They have been invited by governments to take part in ceremonies and official visits all over the world. They have been given a closet's worth of soccer jerseys.

They have changed on the inside, too. Their parents say their sons are more patient and calm. They seem more grown-up and mature, and they show gratitude for small things. The boys themselves say they learned a lot from their rescue. For sure, they are never going anywhere without telling their parents first! But more than that, the experience seems to have broadened their visions for their future. They'd all love to be professional soccer players when they grow up, of course, but now some of the boys imagine becoming Navy SEALs, just like Saman Gunan and the brave men who stayed with them in the darkness. They want to finish school and get good jobs so they can help support their families.

In an interview with ABC News, Adul shares insights about the rescue that show a wisdom far beyond his years: "I want to thank everyone. You loved us, and we also love you all. We feel like we have a lot of parents all around the world, and I wish I could meet you and thank you from the bottom of my heart." He adds, "We are still young and have a lot to learn before we can reach our goals. But we will be good kids, just like everyone wishes us to be. I promise I will try my best."

ALL THIRTEEN

The Wild Boars greet the media for the first time after their release from the hospital.

IT SHOULD NOT HAVE WORKED

AUTHOR'S NOTE

On June 23, 2018, the day the thirteen Wild Boars went missing, my airplane touched down in northern Thailand. I was there on a trip to visit my family, who live in Chiang Mai, just a few hours away from Tham Luang. In fact, we talked about going up to Chiang Rai to visit some caves, but we canceled because the weather didn't look so good. Those same rainstorms that put off our family outing ended up trapping the boys in Tham Luang for eighteen days.

For the rest of our vacation in Thailand, I watched the story of the rescue unfold on 24/7 coverage on Thai TV. (My dad had to translate because I don't speak Thai.) Once the children were found, it was all anyone could talk about. The video that Rick and John shot of the boys when they emerged in Chamber 9 ran on a near constant loop on screens in airports, restaurants, and shopping malls. Even without speaking the language, I felt the sense of worry and hope thick in the air around me. I had to travel back to the United States before the boys were rescued, and, like most of the world, I was glued to my phone, waiting to see if the rescuers could actually make the impossible happen.

Once all thirteen Wild Boars were safely out of the cave, I began seriously thinking about writing this book. I wanted you to learn about this incredible, impossible rescue, and I also wanted to tell you about this incredible place called Thailand. I knew that other books would tell you about Rick and John and the other heroic divers who pulled the boys out of the cave, but I also wanted to tell you about Thanet, and Ay, and the Get-It-Done Crew, and all the thousands of Thai people who were pivotal to saving the boys' lives. I wanted you to know more about the Wild Boars themselves, and why these kids are both extraordinary and totally ordinary at the same time. There are so many lessons to be learned from this rescue. The lesson I wanted to share the most comes from Coach Ek and the boys, who — like their rescuers — defied impossible odds.

They taught me that "impossible" exists only in your mind. You are capable of so much more than you can even imagine.

In early October 2018, I had the happy opportunity to meet all thirteen Wild Boars and their families in person at a dinner hosted by the Royal Thai Consulate General in Los Angeles. The boys had been out of the cave for three months by then. It felt a little surreal to be waiting for their tour bus to pull up — partly because I was extremely jet-lagged, and partly because I had just returned from a research trip during which I had spent the last several weeks talking about these boys.

Just days before, I had been in their hometown of Mae Sai, Thailand, talking with as many people as I could who were involved in the rescue. I met Vern Unsworth, who graciously spent hours tutoring me on everything to do with Tham Luang. I spoke with Ay and the Get-It-Done Crew, Sangwut, and Colonel Singhanat. I went to Wat Doi Wao and met some of the boys' parents and siblings, and I spent time speaking to Phra Khru Prayut, the senior monk there. I visited the site of an enormous mural dedicated to the rescuers, and I paid my respects to a memorial statue of Saman Gunan, standing tall and strong with thirteen wild boars sheltering at his feet.

I made the dusty drive up to Tham Luang, though I couldn't go inside at that time because it was still full of water. Even as this book goes into its second round of edits, seven months after the boys were lost, the cave remains flooded past the Sam Yaek junction. As a mother, my throat clenched tight as I walked across the parking lot, which was once the bustling mission base camp, to the small room where the Wild Boars' parents waited for weeks for their children. I could not imagine looking at that massive mountain of stone every day, knowing that my child was trapped inside, and that I could do nothing to help him except pray and hope.

The author interviews park ranger Nok (left) as rescue worker Ay (right) translates.

Everyone I talked to in Mae Sai still shook their head or pinched the skin of their arms to show me just how impossible the rescue was. No one involved in the operation expected all thirteen boys to make it out. As Vern Unsworth said, "I still can't believe it. It shouldn't have worked. It just should *not* have worked."

But it did. And whether they wanted it or not, the boys have now become world famous. When I met the boys, the Thai government had already received more than two hundred international invitations for the Wild Boars to come visit heads of state, appear on television shows, or be special guests at soccer games! They have received a mountain of presents: soccer jerseys, toys, cleats, and all sorts of trinkets from all over the globe.

I wondered how such instant fame would affect these country boys from Mae Sai. Would they still be able to have normal lives? Their tour bus finally pulled up, an hour late. When the group's escort got off the bus, he apologized. The boys had been having so much fun swimming at the hotel that it was impossible to drag them out of the pool. I smiled. That sounded just about as normal as you could get.

And, of course, the boys were totally normal, regular kids! They were humble and polite, but also goofy and sweet, teasing one another in a friendly way. At one point during a long dinner speech, one of the kids fell asleep in his chair, and his friend waved his fingers in front of his face while the others giggled. Each boy had a family member who had made the trip with him. The parents were so kind and still seemed so relieved to have their children back. They were very happy about the opportunity to travel, but they were also looking forward to going home. No matter how awesome a trip is, there is nothing better than being home with the people you love.

I met Coach Ek, who is cheerful and friendly, and who will talk about soccer at the drop of a hat. To me, he seemed much older and wiser than his twenty-five years. I could definitely understand why the boys felt so close to him and wanted to be like him. I spoke to Adul, who speaks English really well, even though he's too humble to say so. The boys chattered and ate mountains of Thai food and snuggled up next to their parents. I thought they seemed more like a band of brothers than just friends. According to their parents, their ordeal has strengthened their bonds even more. I felt so honored to get to meet them and their families and hear their stories. My favorite story of the Wild Boars, though, is this one:

They had recently attended the Youth Olympic Games, an enormous international event, as guests of honor. Just before they were set to walk out into the crowded stadium, the Wild Boars huddled together to decide how they would come out. True to his style, Coach Ek put the question to the team. Would they wave? Or would they wai (bow)? Or wave and then wai, or what?

It might seem like a small question, but the answer reveals so much about the boys' characters. They discussed and agreed that waving is something that heroes do. They weren't heroes—the people who saved them were the heroes. The boys made a decision together: no waving. They should walk out and wai to show their thanks and humility. That is exactly what they did.

When I heard that story, my heart filled with warmth. I understand why the boys don't want to be called heroes. But I do think they are pretty incredible people. And as long as the world lets them live normal lives, I have a feeling that they will go on to do wonderful things. It sounds as if they are well on their way. The last thing I heard about the Wild Boars is that they are back at home now, back in school, and back at the exact place where they should be: on the soccer field.

The Wild Boars wai to the crowd at a Manchester United soccer game.

ACKNOWLEDGMENTS

The telling of this story is a story all to itself, and there are so many people to thank. To understand this impossible rescue, I first had to understand Tham Luang and caves in general. The first person I reached out to was Martin Ellis, an expert on the caves of Thailand. Martin patiently answered my many questions and also sent me maps and diagrams that helped enormously.

Dr. Marcus Gary of the University of Texas at Austin helped educate me on the geology of karst caves. He also put me in touch with inventor and cave diver Bill Stone, who spent hours telling me hair-raising stories of extreme caving and giving me the scoop on rebreather technology. It was Bill who helped me get in touch with Vern Unsworth.

I can never thank Vern enough for his help in making this book. As one of the only people who have extensively explored Tham Luang, he has been invaluable in helping me understand the cave system and how the rescue unfolded during those early days. Vern has spoken to few journalists about his heroic involvement in the rescue, so I was both surprised and tremendously grateful that he and Tik spent hours speaking with me in Thailand and provided me with maps and photos. I also thank Vern for keeping me updated on all the fascinating developments at Tham Luang since the rescue operation concluded. Not only have Vern and Tik been generous to me as I wrote this book, but they continue to be generous and bighearted members of their community in Mae Sai.

Through them I met so many good people. I am so grateful to Ay, Noi, and Laa for giving me insight into the immense contributions of local Thais to the rescue. Ay introduced me to Nok and to Sangwut, who generously spoke with me and shared photos of the first days of the mission. I also want to thank Nikornchai Phopluechai for sharing so much information (an entire binder's worth!) with me and for providing photos that help tell this story. Thank you to Suwit Jaipom for giving me a detailed tour of the artistic tributes to the rescue, which helped me understand what this event means for the Thai people. I humbly thank Phra Khru Prayut of Wat Doi Wao for helping me understand Coach Ek's character and the role of Buddhism and faith in this story.

My thanks to Major Charles Hodges for speaking with me about the US Air Force's vital role in the rescue. I was so impressed by his leadership and by his team's skill in such an unprecedented crisis. Many thanks to my dear friend Jeff Hasley, who helped me prepare for the interview. I asked Major Hodges the same question I asked every person I interviewed: "What was one aspect of the mission you felt didn't get enough media coverage?" He answered the same as many others: the water.

Luckily, I was able to connect with Thanet Natisri, who so graciously shared his detailed notes and breathtaking photos of his involvement in waging war against the water at Tham Luang. Thanet connected me with Colonel Singhanat, whom I also thank for providing me with vital information for this book.

Many thanks to the content experts who shared their knowledge: social psychologist and group dynamics researcher Dr. Sheryl Bishop, psychiatrist Dr. Armen Goenjian, and cave biologist and sump diver Dr. Jean Krejca, who also provided fascinating photos. Thank you, Cameron Blok-Andersen, CRNA, for helping me understand the use of sedatives during the mission.

Thank you to Thai Navy SEAL commander Chaiyananta Peeranarong for sharing stories of the SEALs' determination and bravery. Thank you to On-usah Chiengkul for all the support and for connecting me with Rear Admiral Apakorn Yuukongkaew. Many thanks to the rear admiral for answering my questions and for giving me permission to use the Thai SEAL photographs for the book.

I am grateful to divers Claus Rasmussen and Ivan Karadzic for their detailed description of the rescue itself. And many thanks to Rob Harper and Rick Stanton for taking the time to answer my questions over email.

My special thanks to the Royal Thai Consulate General and to all the staff in Los Angeles for allowing me to be a part of a special evening with the Wild Boars, and thank you to my uncle Than for the introduction. Thank you to the boys' families for sharing stories of your sons with me. And so many thanks to Coach Ek and to all the boys for speaking with me. It has been an honor to tell your story.

My thanks to Jill Stockton and her fourth-grade classes at Brentwood Elementary for letting me pick their brains about what kids would like to know about this incredible rescue. Thank you to journalist Robert Bradford, who gave me a crash course in conducting interviews. Thank you to Quincy Surasmith for helping me make a book that honors Thailand and its people. Thank you to my fellow nonfiction authors who provided guidance and advice all along the way: Cynthia Levinson, Chris Barton, Loree Griffin Burns, Tracey Baptiste, Martha Brockenbrough, Paige Britt, and Karen Blumenthal. And special thanks to Kate Messner, who helped me so much during the proposal-writing process. Children's book authors truly are the kindest people.

So many thanks to my agent, Stephanie Fretwell-Hill, for being my champion, my confidant, and my wise adviser during this journey. I am so grateful to you and to Karen and Abigail for everything. I cannot thank my editor, Andrea Tompa, enough for all the work she has done for this book. She believed in this story, and in my ability to tell it, from the very beginning. Her dedication to excellence has made it so much stronger. Thank you to Kate Schwartz and Hannah Mahoney, our heroic copyeditors, and to Sherry Fatla, Lisa Rudden, and Karen Minot, for making the book so beautiful inside and out. Thanks to Jamie Tan for taking the book out to the world, and thank you to everyone on the Candlewick team for all you do to put good stories into the hands of children.

My unending love and gratitude to my family. Thank you to my dear Anchalee, Sodsai, Win, and Por for helping your American cousin understand this story from the Thai perspective. Thank you to my uncle Lee for doing anything and going anywhere for family. Thank you to my mother,

Bob, and Liz for your unflagging support, love, and help in raising our girls. How could we do this without you? Thank you to Elowyn and Aven for being troopers while your mom traveled and worked on this book. You inspire me every day. Tom, thank you for our life together. Your love makes anything possible.

Finally, thank you to my dad. Working on this book with you has been one of the proudest accomplishments of my life. You have dedicated your life to me. I dedicate this book to you, even though it can never be enough to thank you for everything you have given me.

SOURCE NOTES

While researching this book, I uncovered more information than I could possibly include. While it was hard to cut out interesting scientific facts and details about the rescue, it was much more difficult to leave out the names of people who worked so hard for the mission's success. For example, though Thanet Natisri led a truly heroic battle against the water at Tham Luang, there were other Thai engineers, geologists, and hydrologists also tackling the problem head-on. Thanet also worked closely with an American rock-climbing instructor who lives in Chiang Mai named Josh Morris, whom I mention only briefly. Josh played a pivotal role in translating and communicating between the international rescue volunteers and the Thai military, and I regret that I wasn't able to tell you more about him.

I regret that I wasn't able to tell you more about everyone! Thousands and thousands of volunteers, mostly Thais, gave their time, money, and energy to the Wild Boars' rescue. If I had the space on the page to tell each of their stories, I gladly would (and this book would weigh a hundred pounds!). For the sake of word count, I have chosen to focus on a few key players in the rescue, but there were so many more who also toiled night and day, giving whatever they could to help get the boys out.

There is a saying in Thailand: Pid thong lung phra. It describes someone who donates money to add gold to a statue in the temple but places their tribute on the back of the statue instead of the front. The phrase honors those who give without the expectation of recognition or reward. There were thousands of people just like this working at Tham Luang. This book is a tribute to all of them.

Much of the information for this book was gathered during my research trip to Mae Sai, Thailand, in October 2018. I am so grateful that my father and my cousins accompanied me on the trip. Not only did they help translate what my Thai-speaking sources said, but they also helped me understand the cultural context and intent of the speakers' words. My father also translated several other sources of information for me, such as the Wild Boars' press conference after their release from hospital. While all quotes in the book refer to actual statements, as is always the case when information is being translated from one language to another, differences can arise between translations. In those cases, I have tried to make the best choices possible. When I met the Wild Boars and their families in Los Angeles on October 11, 2018, staff members of the Thai consulate graciously provided translation for me.

1. A Typical Saturday

p. 2: He's been promising to take . . . outing is still on: "Full News Conference."

p. 2: Being a Wild Boar means . . . local swimming holes: From my conversation with two of the boys' mothers in Los Angeles on October 11, 2018, and from Adul's remarks during the boys' post-temple interview with ABC News, "Exclusive Thai Rescue Interview."

p. 2: On the team's last . . . go there together: "Full News Conference."

p. 2: Some teammates have to . . . and then they'll head back: Ibid.

p. 3: "The Boys of the Wild Boars": Thailand Ministry of Culture, p. 26.

pp. 2, 4: The boys buy snacks . . . before setting out: "Thai Cave Rescue: Birthday Snacks Likely Helped Sustain Footballers During First Days of Ordeal," *Straits Times*, July 4, 2018, https://www.straitstimes.com/asia/se-asia/thai-cave-rescue-birthday-snacks-likely-helped-sustain-footballers-during-first-days-of. This news article, like many others, reported that people and/or family members knew the boys had purchased snacks after their soccer practice. The media assumed that the boys took the snacks with them to the cave. It was only after their rescue that Coach Ek revealed that they had taken no food with them inside Tham Luang.

p. 4: They laugh . . . as they cycle along: Shibani Mahtani, "'It Was Just a Normal Day': Teammate of Trapped Thai Boys Remembers Day His Friends Vanished," *Washington Post*, July 5, 2018, video, https://www.washingtonpost .com/world/asia_pacific/it-was-just-a-normal-day-trapped-thai-teammate -remembers-day-his-friends-vanished/2018/07/05/2eb3f7fc-7fc9-11e8-a63f -7b5d2aba7ac5_story.html.

p. 4: The oldest boys . . . close to Coach Ek, too: This information is taken from conversations I had with several of the boys' parents when I was in Mae Sai in October 2018. While I was there, the Wild Boars were traveling on a goodwill mission to Argentina and the United States. Coach Ek and the three stateless members of the team had just been granted Thai citizenship. Without it, they would not have been able to leave the country. Sadly, their family members were not granted the same rights. This means that while most of the Wild Boars were accompanied by their parents overseas, several of the boys' parents had to stay behind in Thailand. I was able to meet some of these parents at Wat Doi Wao.

p. 4: Adul is the only non-Buddhist . . . all his classes: "'It Was Dark and Quite Scary': Thai Cave Survivors Speak on First Full Day with Families," CBS *This Morning*, July 19, 2018, https://www.youtube.com/watch?v = Hv9sydI7Yjc.

pp. 4–5: "This Is Mae Sai": From discussions with local guides during my research trip to Mae Sai in October 2018.

p. 4: The Wild Boars know . . . focus on school and soccer: During my inter-view with Phra Khru Prayut at Wat Doi Wao on October 4, 2018, he said that the boys are all good, studious students. The boys' parents told me that aside from soccer, they mostly focus on their homework and their studies.

pp. 5–6: Pedaling with him . . . with his big smile: I had the lucky opportunity to meet the Wild Boars and their parents in Los Angeles on October 11, 2018, at the Thai consulate in Los Angeles. At that time, journalists had been discour-aged from asking too many questions about the boys' ordeal inside the cave for fear that it would bring back traumatic memories. Instead, we talked about soccer, travel, and school. It was a wonderful opportunity to learn more about their personalities and their relationships with one another.

The reference to Bew on his moped is based on a video he made on the day, shown with Shibani Mahtani, "'It Was Just a Normal Day': Teammate of Trapped Thai Boys Remembers Day His Friends Vanished," *Washington Post*, July 5, 2018, https://www.washingtonpost.com/world/asia_pacific/it-was-just -a-normal-day-trapped-thai-teammate-remembers-day-his-friends-vanished/2018 /07/05/2eb3f7fc-7fc9-11e8-a63f-7b5d2aba7ac5_story.html.

p. 7: The boys' parents are happy . . . much more than just a coach: Shibani Mahtani, "'He Loved Them More Than Himself': How a 25-Year-Old Former Monk Kept the Thai Soccer Team Alive," *Washington Post*, July 7, 2018, https:// www.washingtonpost.com/world/asia_pacific/he-loved-them-more-than-him self-how-a-25-year-old-former-monk-kept-the-thai-soccer-team-alive/2018/07/07 /b4100076-815e-11e8-b3b5-b61896f90919_story.html.

p. 7: Ek believes . . . boys want the same thing: From my conversation with Coach Ek and the boys' parents in Los Angeles on October 11, 2018, and from Shibani Mahtani, "'He Loved Them More Than Himself': How a 25-Year-Old Former Monk Kept the Thai Soccer Team Alive," *Washington Post*, July 7, 2018, https://www.washingtonpost.com/world/asia_pacific/he-loved-them-more -than-himself-how-a-25-year-old-former-monk-kept-the-thai-soccer-team-alive /2018/07/07/b4100076-815e-11e8-b3b5-b61896f90919_story.html.

p. 7: Tham Luang is only a few miles . . . dark mouth of the cave: From my own visit to Tham Luang in October 2018.

p. 7: Coach Ek leads the boys . . . thin rope and flashlights: "Full News Conference."

p. 7: They walk past a faded sign . . . cave floods at that time: Hannah Beech et al., "'Still Can't Believe It Worked': The Story of the Thailand Cave Rescue," *New York Times*, July 12, 2018, https://www.nytimes.com/2018/07/12/world /asia/thailand-cave-rescue-seals.html.

2. A Sky Full of Water

p. 9: Thailand has three seasons . . . hover for the whole season: "Monsoon Systems," North Carolina State University Climate Office, https://climate.ncsu .edu/edu/Monsoons.

p. 9: the clouds will crack open . . . percent of the year's rainfall: "Thailand Climatological Data," NOAA Central Library, National Oceanic and Atmospheric Administration, https://library.noaa.gov/Collections/Digital-Docs/Foreign -Climate-Data/Thailand-Climate-Data.

p. 10: As soon as the rain stops . . . Land of a Million Rice Fields: Swearer et al., 21.

p. 10: even with preparation . . . landslides in the mountains: Chinnapat Chaimol, "500 Houses Inundated by Flash Flood in Chiang Rai," *Bangkok Post*, July 31, 2018, https://www.bangkokpost.com/news/general/1513198/500 -houses-inundated-by-flash-flood-in-chiang-rai.

p. 10: A changing climate . . . become more extreme: Kendra Pierre-Louis, "Does Climate Change Have Anything to Do with Floods in Thailand?" *New York Times*, July 11, 2018, https://www.nytimes.com/2018/07/11/climate/climate-change -thailand-floods.html.

p. 10: the area around Tham Luang . . . unusually high rain: Author interview with Thanet Natisri, September 23, 2018.

3. The Cave of the Sleeping Lady

p. 13: She is said to have been . . . outline of her face and body: Tassanee Vejpongsa and Keweewit Kaewjinda, "Spirit of Mythical Princess Looms Over Thai Cave Crisis," *Khaosod English*, June 28, 2018, http://www.khaosodenglish.com /featured/2018/06/28/spirit-of-mythical-princess-looms-over-thai-cave-crisis/.

p. 13: For many of the people . . . by the Buddha himself: Swearer et al., 29.

p. 15: A mountain holds power . . . both enticing and dangerous: Andrew Alan Johnson, "Thailand's Caves Are Dangerously Alluring," *The Atlantic*, July 10, 2018, https://www.theatlantic.com/international/archive/2018/07/thailands -caves-are-dangerously-alluring/564806/.

p. 15: Thick stalactite spires . . . flowing curtain of shiny stone: "What Is the Difference Between a Stalactite and a Stalagmite?" Ocean Explorer, National Oceanic and Atmospheric Administration, https://oceanexplorer.noaa.gov /facts/stalactite.html.

p. 15: Twenty feet . . . level of the last flood: Author interview with Major Charles Hodges, commander of the US Air Force 320th Special Tactics Squadron, which advised the Thai government during the rescue, October 29, 2018.

pp. 15, 17: The first 2,000 feet . . . 11 kilometers, away from the entrance: Ellis, 151–152 and 168.

p. 17: a cave is not sterile . . . flowing through the system: Author interview with Vern Unsworth, British caver and expert on the Tham Luang system, October 25, 2018.

p. 18: Suddenly, they come upon a pool . . . the little ones on their backs: "Full News Conference."

p. 18: They have reached a room . . . stop and soak it all in: Author interview with Vern Unsworth, October 25, 2018. Vern told me that after the rescue, he visited Coach Ek in the hospital. Coach recounted their journey back to the Hidden City. Vern was particularly impressed that the boys managed such a long journey in bare feet!

p. 19: Coach Ek says that the cave . . . Tham Luang is flooding: "Full News Conference."

4. First on the Scene

Unless otherwise noted, most of the information in this chapter is taken from my interview with Sangwut Khammongkhon, the head of the Siam Ruam Jai Mae Sai Rescue Organization, on October 8, 2018.

p. 21: Night misses his birthday . . . worry turns to real fear: "Family of Thai Cave Boy Long for Birthday Party Reunion," France 24, July 4, 2018, https://www.france24.com/en/20180704-family-thai-cave-boy-long-birthday-party-reunion.

p. 24: The boys' mothers and fathers . . . I'm waiting for you!": "Against the Elements."

5. Trapped

pp. 27–28: The Wild Boars are only about . . . kicks his legs as they reel him in: "Full News Conference."

p. 28: Coach Ek gets out of the water . . . able to swim out: "Exclusive Thai Cave Rescue Interview."

p. 29: what the boys didn't realize . . . that hit the area a few days before: Author interview with Vern Unsworth, October 5, 2018.

p. 29: The network of tunnels . . . putting white-water rapids to shame: Bill Stone is a super-caver, engineer, cave diver, and inventor who lives in my hometown of Austin, Texas. His expeditions have cracked some of the world's deepest and longest caves. He invented a cave-diving rebreather, a crucial piece of diving equipment used by most high-level cave divers. He has worked with both Rick Stanton and Jason Mallinson, including conducting a grim body recovery with Stanton in Huautla, Mexico. Much of what I learned about how caves flood has come from my conversations with Bill Stone and from his book *Beyond the Deep*, listed in the bibliography.

p. 30: "A Cave Is Born": Author interview with Dr. Marcus Gary, a karst geologist at the University of Texas at Austin, on August 3, 2018, and "An Assessment of Protected Karst Landscapes in Southeast Asia," *Cave and Karst Science* 27, no. 2 (August 2000), 61–70, http://cavescience2-cloud.bcra.org.uk/3_CaveAndKarst Science/cks080.pdf.

pp. 32–33: At 5:00 p.m. on Saturday . . . when they'll be able to get out: "Full News Conference."

6. The Cave Man

I met Vern Unsworth and Tik in Pha Mee, a small mountain town outside Mae Sai, in October 2018. I had been quite surprised that he agreed to an interview, because he is a very private person. He turned out to be one of the most helpful people I spoke with for this book. He brought surveys of the cave to our meeting and drew diagrams of some of the chambers. Vern has an expert knowledge of the cave, which he was so generous (and enthusiastic) about sharing.

p. 36: Some cavers call this experience "scooping . . . treasure to scoop: Stone et al., 264.

p. 37: Based on the elevations . . . about a third of a mile (half a kilometer) past Sam Yaek: Author interview with Vern Unsworth. Vern had told the rescue team that he believed the boys would be found in an elevated area that French explorers had previously named Pattaya Beach. The name of this chamber caused quite a bit of head scratching in Thailand because Pattaya Beach is a coastal town near Bangkok popular with foreign tourists. It seemed a strange name for a room inside a dark cave! There was further confusion later on when it turned out that the place Vern had referred to as Pattaya Beach was actually several hundred meters past the location marked on the French map. News outlets reported that rescue workers were aiming to reach Pattaya Beach, where they hoped to find the boys. In reality, the actual Pattaya Beach chamber did not play a large role in the story, and the boys were sheltering in a different location altogether. Because of all this confusion, I have chosen not to use the name Pattaya Beach in the story or mark it on the maps.

p. 38: "These kids are athletes . . . by continuing to move": Richard C. Paddock, "Divers in Thailand Scour Cave for Missing Soccer Team and Coach," *New York Times*, June 25, 2018, https://www.nytimes.com/2018/06/25/world/asia/thai land-cave-missing-soccer-team.html.

p. 39: "I believe up until . . . abandon each other": Chayut Setboonsarng, "Rescue Teams Battle High Water to Find Boys Missing in Thai Cave," Reuters, June 27, 2018, https://af.reutersmedia.net/article/commoditiesNews/idAFL4N 1TT1BW.

p. 39: The boys' families are emotionally . . . flowers and images of the Buddha: "Flood Waters Hamper Efforts to Rescue Boys Missing in Thai Cave," *The Guardian*, June 25, 2018, https://www.theguardian.com/world/2018/jun/25 /thailand-cave-search-boys-missing-chiang-rai-province. When I met Mark's mother in October 2018, she told me that she fainted every day the boys were in the cave.

p. 39: Hope finally arrives . . . diving gear in tow: "Against the Elements."

pp. 39–40: The SEALs are the country's elite . . . open-water divers in the country: Greg Norman, "Thailand's Versatile, Crime-Fighting Navy SEAL Unit Tasked with Mission to Save Soccer Team Trapped in Cave," *Fox News*, July 6, 2018,

https://www.foxnews.com/world/thailands-versatile-crime-fighting-navy-seal
-unit-tasked-with-mission-to-save-soccer-team-trapped-in-cave; Mayuree
Sukyingcharoenwong, "The Difficult Path to Be a Navy Seal," *The Nation:
Thailand National News*, June 4, 2009, https://web.archive.org/web/201001251
53136/http://www.nationmultimedia.com/2009/06/04/national/national
_30104335.php.

p. 40: The SEALs are such experienced . . . after they retire: Author interview
with Lieutenant Chaiyananta Peeranarong, a former Thai Navy SEAL commander who came out of retirement to offer his diving skills to the rescue
operation, October 30, 2018.

p. 41: The SEALs' commander . . . mission will require: Email correspondence
with On-usah Chiengkul, who served under Admiral Apakorn, November 29,
2018.

p. 41: "I believe they're all . . . good news today": "Divers Enter Flooded Cave
in Search of Missing Students," *Bangkok Post*, June 25, 2018, https://www
.bangkokpost.com/news/general/1492086/divers-enter-flooded-cave-in-search
-of-missing-students.

p. 41: Seeing the SEALs . . . find their children: Author interview with Chaiyon
"Ay" Srisamoot, October 7, 2018. Ay is a sawjaw, an administrative village
leader, who is well connected with many people in Mae Sai.

7. The Dangers of Cave Diving

p. 43: Just before dawn on June 25 . . . wicking away their body heat: This
description is based on photographs posted on the Thai Navy SEAL Facebook
page on June 24, 2018, https://www.facebook.com/ThaiSEAL/photos/a.139315
8180807577/1618933988229994/.

p. 44: One SEAL sticks his foot. . . down the passage: During my interviews with
both Colonel Singhanat, on October 6, 2018, and Sangwut Khammongkhon, on
October 7, 2018, they described how the SEALs pushed through this opening at
Sam Yaek. Thai SEAL captain Anan Surawan also describes it in Lunn.

p. 45: Your skeleton effortlessly . . . atmosphere pressing down on you: Earth's
atmosphere actually extends out more than 6,000 miles (9,700 kilometers) above

the surface of our planet, but most of the air is contained within the first 50 miles (80 kilometers). "Peeling Back the Layers of the Atmosphere," National Oceanic and Atmospheric Administration, February 22, 2016, https://www.nesdis.noaa .gov/content/peeling-back-layers-atmosphere; "Layers of Earth's Atmosphere," Center for Science Education, University Corporation for Atmospheric Research (UCAR), 2015, https://scied.ucar.edu/atmosphere-layers.

p. 45: Even the world's greatest free divers . . . back to the surface: Erin Beresini, "How Long Can Humans Hold Their Breath?" *Outside* online, May 9, 2013, https://www.outsideonline.com/1784106/how-long-can-humans-hold-their -breath.

p. 45: If you keep holding . . . you will drown: Aizita Magaña, "Waiting to Inhale: Why It Hurts to Hold Your Breath," *Science Creative Quarterly*, March 28, 2012, https://www.scq.ubc.ca/waiting-to-inhale-why-it-hurts-to-hold-your -breath/.

p. 46: Dropped lights aren't the only way. . . searching for the way out: This is based on true stories recounted by Sheck Exley in his book *Caverns Measureless to Man*, listed in the bibliography.

p. 47: "Incredibly, despite the lack . . . make the return trip": "Against the Elements." Colonel Singhanat told me during our interview on October 6, 2018, that the SEALs made it about 330 feet (100 meters) past Sam Yaek before having to turn around.

p. 48: In Florida at that time . . . OK to break any of these rules: Exley, *Basic Cave Diving*, 43.

8. Empty Bellies, Clear Minds

p. 51: They've spent the first two days . . . and crying again: When I met some of the boys' parents at Wat Doi Wao in October 2018, they told me that their sons cried during the first two days they were trapped.

p. 51: They scratch messages . . . gives them something to do: Author interview with Vern Unsworth, March 29, 2019. On March 26, 2019, after the cave had drained and dried out, Vern and a small team of volunteers, including Josh Morris, Chaiyon "Ay" Srisamoot, and Mikko Paasi, managed to get back to the chamber where the Wild Boars had been trapped. While exploring the area, they found these messages scratched into the walls of the cave.

p. 51: Bew and Dom tell the others . . . *really* far back: "Full News Conference."

pp. 51–52: Local people tell . . . to his own people: In Mae Sai on October 5, 2018, I interviewed Nikornchai Phopluechai, who operates a local rescue organization and worked at Tham Luang throughout the mission. This story was told to me on the same date by this legendary man's nephew, who works with Nikornchai.

p. 52: The water tastes clean: "Full News Conference."

p. 53: By the third day . . . dreams of food: Ibid.

p. 53: When your body is deprived . . . metabolism to survive: N. G. Norgan, "Adaptations of Energy Metabolism to Level of Energy Intake," Food and Agricultural Organization of the United Nations, October 1981, http://www.fao.org/3/M2997E/M2997E00.htm.

p. 53: It's about 72°F: Email correspondence with Vern Unsworth, January 30, 2019.

p. 53: Coach Ek keeps careful track . . . to get a drink of water: "Full News Conference."

p. 54: The total darkness . . . most frightening of all: Stone, 104. Bill Stone also discussed the Rapture in my conversation with him on September 7, 2018, in Austin, Texas.

p. 55: Coach Ek is determined . . . their own mind: Author interview with Phra Khru Prayut, October 4, 2018. I gained a better understanding of Coach Ek's thoughts on meditation by speaking with his teacher, Phra Khru Prayut, at Wat Doi Wao. I am not a Buddhist myself, though I grew up surrounded by practicing Buddhists and attended Thai temple services often. Julia Cassaniti's book *Living Buddhism*, listed in the bibliography, helped me gain a greater understanding of the beliefs and practices I have observed throughout my life but have never formally studied.

9. At War with the Water

p. 57: It rains heavily . . . Monk's Series passage: Author interview with Vern Unsworth, October 5, 2018.

p. 57: Even though they are almost certain . . . with the current: Author interview with Sangwut Khammongkhon, October 7, 2018.

p. 57: They have set up a communications . . . and extremely reliable: Forester.

p. 58: In the beginning, the pumps . . . generators at the surface: Author interview with Colonel Singhanat, October 6, 2018.

pp. 58–59: From the rate at which it is rising . . . anytime soon is low: During my interview with Vern Unsworth on October 5, 2018, he explained the different sources of water flowing through the cave. Water flowing from both Monk's Series and the main cave passages was a sign to him that the flooding was intensifying.

p. 59: The Thai Navy SEALs again attempt . . . rip his mask off: Hannah Beech et al., "'Still Can't Believe It Worked': The Story of the Thailand Cave Rescue," *New York Times*, July 12, 2018, https://www.nytimes.com/2018/07/12/world/asia/thailand-cave-rescue-seals.html.

p. 59: On June 26 . . . Sam Yaek area completely: Author interview with Vern Unsworth, October 5, 2018.

p. 59: Vern emerges from the cave . . . or the boys will die.": Ibid.

10. The Problem Solvers

The background information in this chapter about Major Hodges and his squadron, the description of his problem-solving techniques, and the account of the rising water in Chamber 1 come from my interview with him on October 29, 2018, and from the interview he gave to the *Patriot to the Core* podcast (see Forester in the bibliography).

p. 61: His squadron quickly assembles . . . on the evening of June 27: Hope Hodge Seck, "'Expecting Casualties': How Airmen Created the Incredible Thai

Cave Rescue Plan," Military.com, September 25, 2018, https://www.military.com/daily-news/2018/09/25/expecting-casualties-how-airmen-created-incredible-thai-cave-rescue-plan.html.

p. 63: The first option is to drill . . . pulling them up to the surface: Joseph Stromberg, "The Capsule That Saved the Chilean Miners," *Smithsonian*, January 2012, https://www.smithsonianmag.com/innovation/the-capsule-that-saved-the-chilean-miners-5620851/.

p. 63: Locals insist . . . they have to give this third option a shot: In my interview with Vern Unsworth on October 5, 2018, he stated that he knew there would be no alternative entrances into Tham Luang, but he felt he had to help follow the leads given by local people.

p. 64: Members of Thailand's national parks . . . the overland search: "Underwater Robot, Airborne Drones Aid Cave Search," *Bangkok Post*, June 26, 2018, https://www.bangkokpost.com/news/general/1492678/underwater-robot-airborne-drones-aid-cave-search.

p. 64: thousands of volunteers . . . from Australia and China: "Thailand Cave Rescue Efforts Pick Up Pace as Flooding Eases," *Voice of America*, June 30, 2018, https://www.voanews.com/a/thailand-cave-rescue-efforts-pick-up-pace-as-flooding-eases/4461538.html.

p. 64: These guides are highland indigenous . . . and quite isolated from one another: "Thailand: Highland Indigenous Peoples," Minority Rights Group International, https://minorityrights.org/minorities/highland-ethnic-groups/.

p. 64: Among the many volunteers . . . pitch-black shafts: "Thai Cave Rescue: Bird's Nest Collectors Scour for Ways into Cave to Save Youth Footballers," *Straits Times*, July 5, 2018, https://www.straitstimes.com/asia/se-asia/thai-cave-rescue-birds-nest-collectors-scour-for-ways-into-cave-to-save-youth.

p. 64: Governor Narongsak sends . . . and take photographs: "Flood Waters Hamper Efforts to Rescue Boys Missing in Thai Cave," *The Guardian*, June 25, 2018, https://www.theguardian.com/world/2018/jun/25/thailand-cave-search-boys-missing-chiang-rai-province.

pp. 64–65: The searchers find some shafts . . . a dead end: Forester.

p. 65: When the search teams are still . . . and sleep in the forest: Author interview with Chaiyon "Ay" Srisamoot, October 7, 2018.

pp. 65–66: Back at base camp . . . spirit of the cave: "Distraught Relatives Turn to Prayer Ceremony as Rescue Teams Continue Search for 12 Missing Football Players," *Chiang Rai Times*, June 26, 2018, https://www.chiangraitimes.com /distraught-relatives-turn-to-prayer-ceremony-as-rescue-teams-continue-search -for-12-missing-football-players.html.

p. 66: People play gongs and beat drums . . . the lost boys from the cave: "Underwater Robot, Airborne Drones Aid Cave Search," *Bangkok Post*, June 26, 2018, https://www.bangkokpost.com/news/general/1492678/underwater-robot -airborne-drones-aid-cave-search.

pp. 66–67: The families are joined . . . go back to normal: "Parents on Edge as Rain Hinders Hunt," *Bangkok Post*, June 27, 2018, https://www.bangkokpost .com/news/general/1492834/parents-on-edge-as-rain-hinders-hunt; "'It Was Just a Normal Day': Teammate of Trapped Thai Boys Remembers Day His Friends Vanished," *Washington Post*, July 5, 2018, https://www.washingtonpost.com /world/asia_pacific/it-was-just-a-normal-day-trapped-thai-teammate-remembers -day-his-friends-vanished/2018/07/05/2eb3f7fc-7fc9-11e8-a63f-7b5d2aba7ac5 _story.html; Steve George, "Thailand Cave Rescue: Friends Say Boys Ignored Warnings," CNN, July 5, 2018, https://www.cnn.com/2018/07/05/asia/thailand -cave-town-intl/index.html.

pp. 68–69: But then base camp . . . can they deny this?: "Monk Who Predicted Thai Cave Rescue Hailed for Intervention," *The Irrawaddy*, July 3, 2018, https:// www.irrawaddy.com/news/burma/monk-predicted-thai-cave-rescue-hailed -intervention.html; "A Mystical Take on the Thai Cave Rescue," *Bangkok Post*, July 4, 2018, https://www.bangkokpost.com/news/general/1497458/a-mystical -take-on-the-tham-luang-cave-rescue. When I spoke to Mae Sai locals, including some of the boys' parents, they attributed much of the mission's success to Kruba Boonchum's presence and intervention.

p. 69: Major Hodges gives the families space . . . anyone in the rescue: Forester.

p. 69: His commanding officer calls . . . find their remains": Author interview with Major Hodges, October 29, 2018.

p. 69: The Thai air force has just deployed . . . flooded entrance passages:

"Underwater Robot, Airborne Drones Aid Cave Search," *Bangkok Post*, June 26, 2018, https://www.bangkokpost.com/news/general/1492678/underwater -robot-airborne-drones-aid-cave-search.

p. 69: So far, no one . . . and keep going: This explanation of the limitations of amphibious robots was given to me by Bill Stone, who designs underwater robots, on September 7, 2018.

11. The Sump Divers

pp. 71–72: When Vern Unsworth warned . . . trio of British amateurs: Author interview with Vern Unsworth, October 5, 2018. Vern told me that the Thai authorities put off his request for help from the BCRC three times before he was able to persuade them to put the call through. He partially attributed their reluctance to their skepticism that an amateur cave diver could have more experience than their military divers. But he also acknowledged that his blunt and assertive communication style likely didn't serve him well with the Thai leadership.

p. 72: Thailand's most elite military . . . China, and Australia: "Thailand Cave Rescue Efforts Pick Up Pace as Flooding Eases," *Voice of America*, June 30, 2018, https://www.voanews.com/a/thailand-cave-rescue-efforts-pick-up-pace -as-flooding-eases/4461538.html.

p. 72: This is also what happens . . . gradually drain away: Author interview with Bill Stone, September 7, 2018.

pp. 72–73: For cavers, a sump is a major bummer . . . and record setting: Farr. I learned so much about the history of cave diving and the mentality of divers from Farr's book *The Darkness Beckons*, listed in the bibliography.

p. 73: The BCRC is a group of . . . support the pair aboveground: Sharon Wheeler, "Behind the Scenes with the BCRC at the Thai Cave Rescue—Part One," Darkness Below, September 9, 2018, https://darknessbelow.co.uk/unsung-heroes-the -backroom-story-of-the-thai-cave-rescue-part-one/; "About Cave Rescue" and "How Cave Rescue Works," British Cave Rescue Council, http://www.cave rescue.org.uk/about-cave-rescue/ and http://www.caverescue.org.uk/about -cave-rescue/how-cave-rescue-works/.

p. 73: They hold a good share . . . push them forward: "Rick Stanton," *Diver*,

October 2007, http://archive.divernet.com/cave-diving/p302428-rick-stanton. html. See also *The Darkness Beckons*, by Martyn Farr (listed in the bibliography), which recounts multiple stories about Rick and John's accomplishments and adventures together.

pp. 73–74: Rick, John, and Rob arrive . . . to the cave: Author interview with Woranan "Tik" Ratrawiphakkun, October 5, 2018. I had the pleasure of meeting Tik during my research trip to Thailand, where she explained all the many tasks and responsibilities she undertook to support the rescue.

p. 74: Journalists surround them . . . a job to do": Lunn.

p. 74: They hope to get a good look . . . scramble for the exit: Author interview with Vern Unsworth, October 25, 2018. According to Vern, this episode was actually quite scary. Vern had taken Rick, John, and Rob inside to have a look at the cave. The sump between Chambers 2 and 3 had water in it but was not yet flooded. Vern says that the sound of water rushing inside the cave became louder and louder, and the water suddenly began rising before their eyes. They had to rush out quickly, and Rob Harper, who was the farthest back in the cave, had to make a mad dash for it!

pp. 74–75: The next day . . . about being electrocuted: Vern and Tik told me this was a real worry of Rick's and John's given how much electrical equipment was submerged underwater.

pp. 75–77: The water is a cloudy . . . deeper and swim even farther: The story of the men unexpectedly rescued by Rick and John did not become public until Rick recounted it during a lecture at the Hidden Earth conference in September 2018, as reported in Tony Brocklebank, "Breaking News: British Cave Divers Also Rescued Four Trapped Thai Rescuers in Tham Luang Cave," Darkness Below, September 24, 2018, https://darknessbelow.co.uk/breaking-news-british -cave-divers-also-rescued-four-trapped-thai-rescuers-in-tham-luang-cave/. See also Kaweewit Kaewjinda, "Hapless Helpers Recount Own Rescue by Divers from Thai Cave," Associated Press, September 26, 2018, https://www.apnews.com /22fcc19fb54344609fde9deb50f0aa23.

Regarding the reference to the experience being sobering for Rick and John, in Craig Challen's lecture listed in the bibliography, he says that the near-panicking behavior of the Thai workers during the snatch rescue emphasized to Rick and John how difficult it would be dive out the children without having them succumb to panic.

12. Coach Ek

p. 79: The Wild Boars are resting . . . or three meters": "Full News Conference." At the conference, the boys and Coach Ek did not indicate what day the water rose up so quickly. Based on the events recounted by the rescuers such as Vern Unsworth, I assume that this sudden flood happened on either June 26 or June 27, because those are the two days when flooding began to intensify.

p. 79: relatively flat space the size of a small bedroom: Author interview with Vern Unsworth, March 26, 2019.

pp. 79–80: Before, it had seemed . . . are doubly trapped: The explanation for the source of the flooding comes from my interview with Vern Unsworth, October 5, 2018.

p. 80: Even in their perilous state . . . others where they are: The boys' mothers told me about the boys' promise to one another when I met them on October 11, 2018.

p. 80: One thing that keeps . . . people they love: After the boys recuperated, they took part in some art therapy sessions with local artists. I met Suwit Jaipom, the president of the Art Bridge Chiang Rai Foundation, who showed me the drawings and sculptures the boys made to express their thoughts when they were inside the cave. Every child drew pictures of his family.

p. 80: Coach Ek has few . . . in the Shan region: Reuters reported that Coach Ek is of Tai Lue descent (Panu Wongcha-um and Patpicha Tanakasempipat, "Coach of Rescued Thai Soccer Team a 'Country Boy' Longing for Citizenship," Reuters, July 12, 2018, https://www.reuters.com/article/us-thailand-accident-cave-coach /coach-of-rescued-thai-soccer-team-a-country-boy-longing-for-citizenship-idUSK BN1K21H8). The Tai Lue are one of the highland indigenous peoples who have made their homes in the mountains of northern Thailand, Myanmar, and southern China. However, the *New York Times* reported that Coach Ek was of the Shan minority (Hannah Beech, "Stateless and Poor, Some Boys in Thai Cave Had Already Beaten Long Odds," *New York Times*, July 10, 2018, https:// www.nytimes.com/2018/07/10/world/asia/thailand-cave-soccer-stateless.html). Through my own research, I did not find clarification on this matter beyond that he most likely hails from the Shan region of Myanmar, which is home to thirty-three distinct ethnic groups ("Shan," Minority Rights Group International, https://minorityrights.org/minorities/shan/).

p. 80: Migrant children face tough . . . addicted to drugs: "UNICEF Thailand Annual Report 2018," UNICEF, p. 8, https://www.unicef.org/thailand/reports /unicef-thailand-annual-report-2018. The devastating effects of the drug trade on Thai communities is well documented, such as by the International Conference on Public Policy.

p. 80: At the age of nine . . . almost eleven years: The story of Ek's life in the temple before he became a coach for the Wild Boars was told to me by his mentor, Phra Khru Prayut, when I visited Wat Doi Wao on October 4, 2018.

Some newspaper articles, such as "Thai Cave Boys: The Story Behind Coach Ekkapol Chantawong," *Australian*, July 4, 2018, reported that Coach Ek has family living in the area. But Phra Khru Prayut told me that Ek has no family except for his grandmother. He said that once the rescue became big news, many people came to the temple claiming to be his family and offering a place for him to live. But in the four years that Ek lived at Wat Doi Wao, no family ever visited him. There may also have been some confusion in the media caused by the Thai custom of calling an elder woman "Aunt" even if she is not a true relative.

p. 82: Coach Ek and three other members . . . many of them children: "Thailand," International Observatory on Statelessness, http://www.national ityforall.org/thailand.

p. 82: Many of those who cross . . . and sleeping on the other: Mae Sai is right on the border between Thailand and Myanmar, and I was able to see this daily crossing of migrant workers during my trip there.

p. 82: Violence and persecution . . . across the border seeking safety: "Shan," Minority Rights Group International, https://minorityrights.org/minorities/shan/.

p. 82: Other groups, such as the Rohingya . . . continued violence and even death: "MSF Surveys Estimate That at Least 6,700 Rohingya Were Killed During the Attacks in Myanmar," Médecins Sans Frontières, December 12, 2017, https:// www.msf.org/myanmarbangladesh-msf-surveys-estimate-least-6700-rohingya -were-killed-during-attacks-myanmar; Supalak Ganjanakhundee, "Thailand's Refusal to Recognise Rohingya as Refugees Leaves Them in Illegal Limbo," *The Nation/Thailand*, March 4, 2018, https://www.nationmultimedia.com/detail /asean-plus/30340157; Nikki Ostrand, "The Stateless Rohingya in Thailand," Center for Migration Studies, https://cmsny.org/the-stateless-rohingya-in -thailand/.

p. 82: Stateless people in Thailand . . . statelessness continues: "Blood, Soil, and Paper: Thailand's Mission to Reduce Statelessness," *The Conversation*, August 2, 2018, https://theconversation.com/blood-soil-and-paper-thailands -mission-to-reduce-statelessness-100519.

p. 83: Thailand has pledged to reduce . . . slowed the reform process: "Thailand," International Observatory on Statelessness, http://www.nationalityforall.org /thailand.

p. 83: Some people, such as Wild Boar team member Adul . . . makes them want to excel": Hannah Beech, "Stateless and Poor, Some Boys in Thai Cave Had Already Beaten Long Odds," *New York Times*, July 10, 2018, https:// www.nytimes.com/2018/07/10/world/asia/thailand-cave-soccer-stateless.html.

pp. 84–85: He impressed the senior monk . . . It was home: Phra Khru Prayut spoke at length about Coach Ek's heart and character.

pp. 85–86: Aside from his Buddhist faith . . . like a dream coming true: The information about Ek's personal life is taken from my conversation with him in Los Angeles on October 12, 2018, and my interview with Phra Khru Prayut on October 4, 2018.

p. 86: About 488 million people . . . Buddhists today: "Buddhists," Pew Research Center, December 18, 2012, https://www.pewforum.org/2012/12/18/global -religious-landscape-buddhist/. I learned more about the history and importance of Buddhist temples in Thailand in Julia Cassaniti's book *Living Buddhism*, listed in the bibliography.

p. 87: In the nain ceremony . . . first challenge!: My father and cousins have served as novice monks several times in Thailand. They have passed on their stories about ordination, the difficulties of adjusting to monastic life, and the many lessons they learned.

p. 87: Keep fighting: This is a common phrase and sentiment in Thailand, used to help keep someone's spirits up. In the ABC News exclusive interview with the Wild Boars on August 23, 2018, the boys say how they told one another to "keep fighting."

13. The Water Expert

Thanet Natisri kept a detailed diary of his experience helping with the Tham Luang rescue, and he graciously shared it with me. Unless otherwise noted, this chapter is constructed from his diary and from our conversations on September 22, 25, and 28, 2018.

p. 89: The ditch along the roadside . . . being pumped out of the cave: I saw this ditch when I visited Tham Luang, and our guide pointed out that it had been full of water during the rescue.

p. 89: He learned about working with groundwater . . . company in Thailand: Thanet Natisri's father-in-law, Veera Vasinvarthana, also consulted on tackling the water management at Tham Luang.

p. 95: The homemade super-pumps are nicknamed . . . beast in Thai mythology: Author interview with Colonel Singhanat, October 6, 2018.

p. 95: The farmers explain that . . . taken them up on their offer: "Against the Elements."

14. The Rescue Stalls

p. 97: The parents bring their sons' clothing . . . where the boys are located: "The Thai Cave Rescue: Drones, Dogs, Drilling, and Desperation," BBC News, June 30, 2018, https://www.bbc.com/news/world-asia-44652397.

pp. 98–99: A dead body requires a recovery . . . extracting their body even trickier: Stone et al., 169. In this passage, Bill Stone describes the difficult body recovery of Rick's fellow diver and friend Ian Rolland, who died deep in the Huautla cave in Mexico in 1994. The stalwart way Rick approached the harrowing task reveals quite a bit about both his mental and physical strength.

p. 99: They think it's foolish . . . won't listen to them about the risks: This lack of understanding between the UK divers and the Thai authorities was described to me by Vern Unsworth, October 5, 2018, and by diver Claus Rasmussen, October 18, 2018.

p. 99: Relationships between the diving team . . . getting them out:

Disagreements and tension between the UK dive team and the Thai authorities were described to me by several of the people I interviewed. I never had the opportunity to interview Governor Narongsak for his own take on these disagreements. Ultimately, after speaking to dozens of rescuers of different nationalities, my takeaway is that despite many differences, all members of the rescue team were united in their goal, and this is what ultimately allowed the mission to succeed.

pp. 99–101: Ben Reymenants, a Belgian diver . . . see what the next day will bring: Reymenants, who played a large role in laying guidelines inside Tham Luang during the rescue, asserted in his interview to BBC Radio on July 12, 2018, that Rick and John had given up on the rescue because of the conditions and were packing up to go home. Vern Unsworth and Major Charles Hodges both told me that Rick and John had not thrown in the towel completely, though on June 29 and June 30 the conditions were so awful that it seemed unlikely that diving would be possible. Major Hodges had great respect for their assessment of the risks involved. My interview with Claus Rasmussen on October 18, 2018, illuminated some details about this event as well.

p. 100: "Stay Cool": The cultural differences between the Western rescuers and Thai leadership, and how this impacted the rescue, was discussed by both Thanet Natisri and Claus Rasmussen in my interviews with them. Claus, who has lived in Thailand for fifteen years and whose wife and children are Thai, believed the differences in cultural norms contributed to the tense relations between the camps.

15. The Beautiful Game

p. 103: The water flowing through the cave . . . straight from the stream: "Full News Conference."

p. 103: For the first couple of days, the boys . . . they just pee downstream: Author interview with Vern Unsworth, March 29, 2019. On March 28, 2019, Vern Unsworth made his second trip back to the chamber where the boys had been trapped. Along with a small group of people who had participated in the rescue and some Thai SEALs, Vern was there to carry out some of the SEALs' equipment that had been left in the cave. As he was hiking in, he was shocked to realize that one of the Wild Boars was part of the group! Mix had come back with a friend to retrieve one of his flashlights that had been left inside. Contrary to what I would expect, he was not at all anxious or traumatized to reenter the cave. While they were back in Chamber 9, he described to Vern where the team stayed and where they went to the "bathroom."

p. 103: The boys have all started to lose . . . death is not far behind: Leach, 90.

p. 104: If your temperature dips . . . cause your heart to fail: "Hypothermia," Mayo Clinic, https://www.mayoclinic.org/diseases-conditions/hypothermia /symptoms-causes/syc-20352682.

p. 104: The Wild Boars are luckily not submerged . . . their clothes and skin: Having gone caving in wet caves myself, I know from experience how difficult it is to stay dry inside one. This problem is also described in Stone et al. and Tabor.

p. 104: Thi sets his watch with two . . . a regular schedule: From conversations with the boys' parents in Thailand.

p. 104: even when they're huddled . . . hallucinations can occur: Walker, 3–7.

p. 104: This is a phrase . . . successfully on the other side: Leach, 149–169 and 173–175.

p. 105: "Stages of Hypothermia": Lynne McCullough and Sanjay Arora, "Diagnosis and Treatment of Hypothermia," *American Family Physician* 70 (December 15, 2004), no. 12: 2325–2332.

p. 107: Every soccer player at every level . . . and leave it all on the field: I love watching and playing soccer for fun. But while I have played other team sports, I have never played soccer at a competitive level myself. This description of how it feels to give it your all during a soccer match is based on conversations with friends and family members who played competitive soccer in their youth.

p. 107: Coach Ek knows that he . . . not giving up the game: "Full News Conference."

16. Going Back In

p. 109: Schools hold special assemblies . . . *let them be alive*: "Nation Prays for

Safe Return of Team," *Bangkok Post*, June 29, 2018, https://www.bangkokpost
.com/news/general/1494146/nation-prays-for-safe-return-of-team.

p. 110: No one wants to speak out loud . . . are most likely dead: This sentiment
was communicated to me by Ay and his friends during our conversations in
Mae Sai. No one that I interviewed other than Phra Khru Prayut and the boys'
families believed that the children would be found alive at this point during the
rescue.

p. 110: At Sai Tong, Thanet stands in water . . . each day out of Sai Tong cave:
Author interview with Thanet Natisri, September 25, 2018.

p. 110: it floods over 550 acres . . . whom they think of as their own family:
"Against the Elements."

pp. 110–111: On the morning of Sunday . . . going to take advantage of it:
Author interview with Thanet Natisri, September 25, 2018.

p. 111: The water has lowered enough that . . . wading through waist-deep water:
Ryn Jirenuwat and Richard C. Paddock, "Thailand Rescuers Report Progress in
Search for Soccer Team," *New York Times*, July 1, 2018, https://www.nytimes
.com/2018/07/01/world/asia/thailand-cave-soccer-boys.html.

p. 113: When the divers resurface in Chamber 3 . . . he tells journalists: Ryn
Jirenuwat and Richard C. Paddock, "Thailand Rescuers Report Progress in
Search for Soccer Team," *New York Times*, July 1, 2018, https://www.nytimes
.com/2018/07/01/world/asia/thailand-cave-soccer-boys.html.

p. 113: The forecast shows relatively dry . . . to find the boys is extremely short:
Author interview with Thanet Natisri, September 25, 2018.

17. Creating a Diversion

Unless otherwise noted, this chapter is based on what I learned from Thanet
Natisri during our interviews and from his rescue diary.

p. 121: Every day, the medical tent . . . hobbled down from the mountain:
Nikornchai Phopluechai supervised one of the medical tents at Tham Luang,
and he told me that minor injuries were a daily and frequent occurrence.

18. One Last Try

I learned how rebreathers work by reading about the inventor of the commercial diving rebreather, Bill Stone, in his book *Beyond the Deep*, listed in the bibliography. Farr and Tabor also have great information about the development of rebreather technology.

p. 124: Rick Stanton likes to keep . . . out of a rubber doormat: "Rick Stanton," *Diver*, October 2007, http://archive.divernet.com/cave-diving/p302428-rick -stanton.html.

pp. 124–125: The rebreather Rick designed . . . well as any computer: Author interview with Bill Stone, September 7, 2018. His exact words were "The guy could dive on a refrigerator."

pp. 123, 126: Rick Stanton has a pre-dive ritual . . . a sump diver must have: Tabor, 146.

p. 126: That laser focus on the present . . . want to stay alive: E. R. Straughan, "Touched by Water: The Body in Scuba Diving." *Emotion, Space, and Society* 5 (February 2012), 19–26.

p. 127: It doesn't take long . . . the smell of human feces: "Rick Stanton Gives Incredible Account of Thai Cave Rescue." In this ITV interview, Rick was a bit polite and didn't quite describe what the smell was, but in speaking with me, Vern Unsworth made no bones about what it was! Vern also told me that Rick's first thought was that he was smelling a decomposing body. The rescuers were prepared to find that at least one of the boys had died.

19. "Brilliant"

Unless otherwise noted, this chapter is based on statements given by the boys and Coach Ek during their post-hospital press conference ("Full News Conference"), and during an interview granted to ABC News after they completed their service at Wat Doi Wao ("Exclusive Thai Cave Rescue Interview"). The dialogue between the boys and the divers is quoted from the video footage posted on the Thai Navy SEALs' Facebook page on July 2, 2018, which my father helped translate (https://www.facebook.com/ThaiSEAL/videos/163122 8493667210/).

p. 129: The team has become used to . . . whir of helicopter blades: At Wat Doi Wao, the boys' family members told me that their sons heard helicopters and animals when they meditated, and this gave them hope that someone would find them.

p. 129: The constant echo . . . there is no one nearby: According to Vern Unsworth, this is a common phenomenon that cavers experience.

p. 132: The men explain that Thai Navy SEALs . . . and a doctor with them: According to Major Hodges, the US military did not have any idea that the Thai SEALs would dive back to the Wild Boars the following day. It's possible that Rick and John were merely trying to be positive and encouraging when they told the boys that SEALs were coming with supplies the next day.

p. 133: Before Rick and John depart . . . is not the norm: Rick Stanton told Vern Unsworth that the boys hugged them before they left Chamber 9, and Vern relayed this to me via text message. In January 2019, Rick told me that could not remember whether the boys instigated the hugging or whether John Volanthen did. The description of hugging in Thai culture is based on my own experiences and on discussions about this with my family.

p. 133: By hugging Rick and John . . . become like family: The Wild Boars made a guest appearance on the UK's ITV *This Morning* in October 2018, along with some of their rescuers. In a short speech that left even the stoic rescuers teary-eyed, Coach Ek thanked them for their sacrifice and told them that he and the boys consider them like family ("Thai Cave Survivors Reunited with British Rescue Divers," ITV This Morning, October 30, 2018, https://www.youtube.com/watch?v = wTCFwjjaaMg).

p. 133: The dive through the cave . . . are two very different things": Rosemary E. Lunn, "Thailand Cave Rescue: John Volanthen Speaks," *X-Ray Magazine*, July 14, 2018, https://xray-mag.com/content/thailand-cave-rescue-john-volanthen-speaks.

20. Now What?

p. 135: Governor Narongsak is with . . . actually be good news?: "All Children, Coach Found Alive in Cave." *Khaosod English*, July 2, 2018, http://www.khao

sodenglish.com/news/crimecourtscalamity/calamity/2018/07/02/all-children
-coach-rescued-from-cave/.

p. 136: The Wild Boars are two miles . . . below the surface: "Thai Cave Rescue."

pp. 136–137: Every option for rescuing them . . . pumps will likely be overwhelmed once more: Forester.

pp. 137–138: As soon as Rick and John emerge . . . were sure their comrades
had died: This story of why and how the Thai SEALs and Dr. Pak ended up in
Chamber 9 was told to me separately by both Vern Unsworth and Major Hodges
and recounted in the "Against the Elements" documentary, listed in the bibliography. Dr. Pak describes his terrifying experience diving into Tham Luang in
an interview with Thai Visa News, "SEAL Rescuer Dr. Pak Recalls 'Close Shave
with Death' Inside Tham Luang Cave," September 23, 2018, https://thaipbs
world.com/seal-rescuer-dr-park-recalls-close-shave-with-death-inside-tham
-luang-cave.

pp. 138–139: "I told myself that . . . as long as it took": "Full News Conference."

p. 139: The boys have been dreaming . . . rice and a fried egg: Ibid.

p. 139: The first food the Thai SEALs bring . . . something they have all been
craving: Author interview with Chaiyon "Ay" Srisamoot, October 7, 2018. These
two foods were procured by Ay and his team.

p. 139: On July 4, Rick and John . . . Meals, Ready to Eat: Author interview
with Major Hodges, October 29, 2018. MREs and their contents are described
on the US Army website, https://www.goarmy.com/soldier-life/fitness-and
-nutrition/components-of-nutrition/meals-ready-to-eat.html.

p. 140: Halfway up the hill in Chamber 9 . . . to the top of the slope: Author
interview with Vern Unsworth, March 29, 2019.

p. 140: One of the SEALs in particular . . . teasing, mostly by him: "Full News
Conference."

p. 140: The boys had misunderstood . . . there to boost morale: Adul describes
this misunderstanding in the post-temple interview the team gave to ABC News
("Exclusive Thai Cave Rescue Interview").

p. 140: "Really strong composure": Jason Mallinson in "Out of the Dark," transcript, p. 13.

p. 141: Thailand's tourism tagline is "The Land of Smiles" . . . and to keep cool yourself: This description is based on my own experiences in Thailand and conversations with my family and other friends about smiling in Thai culture. In most interviews I have found with the British and Australian divers who interacted with the boys while they were still trapped in Tham Luang, they remark on how surprised they were to see the Wild Boars smiling. Thai people were also heartened by the boys' positivity, but I felt that they were less shocked to see the boys smiling. In fact, when I called one of my Thai cousins to ask her thoughts on this, her response was "Of course they were smiling! They were nervous. What do you do when you're nervous? You smile!" I thought this was a nice illustration of the different expectations Thais and Westerners might have had for how the children would behave.

p. 141: The SEALs record a video . . . need to come home: Video posted to the Thai Navy SEAL Facebook page, July 3, 2018, https://www.facebook.com/Thai SEAL/videos/1634041306719262.

21. The Get-It-Done Crew

Unless otherwise noted, the information in this chapter comes from my conversations with Ay, Noi, Laa, Tik, and Nok, whom I was able to meet and interview during my trip to Thailand in October 2018.

p. 143: The mountain now swells with ten thousand people: Hannah Beech et al., "'Still Can't Believe It Worked': The Story of the Thailand Cave Rescue," *New York Times*, July 12, 2018, https://www.nytimes.com/2018/07/12/world /asia/thailand-cave-rescue-seals.html.

p. 146: The king of Thailand has been monitoring . . . the rescuers sorely need: Muktita Suhartono and Richard C. Paddock, "Soccer Team Is Found Alive in Thailand Cave Rescue," *New York Times*, July 2, 2018, https://www.nytimes .com/2018/07/02/world/asia/thailand-boys-rescued.html.

22. Panic

p. 149: If they do end up diving . . . not just anyone will do: Sharon Wheeler, "Behind the Scenes with the BCRC at the Thai Cave Rescue—Part One," Darkness Below, September 9, 2018, https://darknessbelow.co.uk/unsung -heroes-the-backroom-story-of-the-thai-cave-rescue-part-one/; "Tham Luang Nang Non Cave, Thailand—Update," British Cave Rescue Council, July 5, 2018, https://www.caverescue.org.uk/tham-luang-nang-non-cave-thailand-update-4/.

p. 150: Some of the first divers . . . in the Western Hemisphere: Jason Mallinson, Rick Stanton, John Volanthen, and Dutch cave diver René Houben share the world record for the longest cave dive: 28,871 feet (8,800 meters).

p. 150: *These kids are not going to make it out*: "Out of the Dark," transcript, p. 6. During an interview in the film with Mark Willacy, Jason Mallinson said, "The first thought is they're not going to get out."

p. 150: The news media at this time . . . none of the boys know how to swim: For some reason, this detail seemed to make it into almost every news story at the time. It's not true. According to their parents, all the boys knew how to swim, though some were weaker swimmers than others.

p. 150: "Panic is a knife's edge . . . impossible to bring yourself out of it": Author interview with Bill Stone, September 7, 2018.

pp. 150–151: Even experienced divers have succumbed . . . yank your regulator out of your mouth: Exley, *Caverns Measureless to Man*. Sheck Exley's book is full of incredible stories of scrapes with death while cave diving. Even though he truly is the "King of Calm," he does not disparage those who panic underwater, stating that it's a natural human reaction to the extreme circumstances.

p. 151: The space exploration company . . . for the passenger inside: Ashley Wong, "Elon Musk Sends an 'Escape Pod' to Help in Thai Cave Rescue," *USA Today*, July 9, 2018, https://www.usatoday.com/story/tech/2018/07/09/elon -musk-sends-escape-pod-help-thai-cave-rescue/768988002/; Muktita Suhartono and Julia Jacobs, "Thai Navy May Put Elon Musk's Mini-Submarine to Use. One Day," *New York Times*, July 12, 2018, https://www.nytimes.com/2018/07/12 /world/asia/elon-musk-thai-cave-submarine-nyt.html. Craig Challen describes the capsule's lack of gas monitoring in Challen, "Thai Cave Rescue."

pp. 152–154: short notes for their parents . . . happy moment for the kids and their families: "Cave Rescue: Thai Boys and Parents Send Letters of Love and Reassurance," BBC News, July 7, 2018, https://www.bbc.com/news/world-asia -44748927. I used my father's translation of these letters, which differs slightly from this article's translation. Jason Mallinson described his idea to bring notes in and out of the cave in "Out of the Dark," transcript, p. 12.

p. 154: Air-quality meters . . . around 15 percent: Kocha Olarn et al., "Thai Cave Rescuers Face Race Against Time as Oxygen Levels Drop," CNN, July 6, 2018, https://www.cnn.com/2018/07/05/asia/thai-cave-diver-intl/index.html; Challen. In Challen's lecture, he expresses skepticism that the oxygen levels in Chamber 9 had actually dropped this low. He claims that he did not detect any noticeable dip in the oxygen levels when he dived back to the boys. He also notes that when water actively runs through a cave, it carries oxygen in with it from the surface and absorbs carbon dioxide, serving as a sort of natural air filter. Expert caver Bill Stone expressed this same skepticism to me when I interviewed him. It is possible that the oxygen meters gave a wrong reading or had not been properly calibrated. Regardless of the true level, the belief that the boys were running out of oxygen in Chamber 9 was a significant factor driving decisions about their rescue.

p. 154: Even healthy adults find it hard . . . pass out and can die: Edward Naranjo, "Oxygen Deficiency: The Silent Killer," EHS Today, December 1, 2007, https://www.ehstoday.com/fire_emergencyresponse/ehs_imp_77598.

p. 155: The Thais have a plan . . . tragedy has struck inside Tham Luang: Author interview with Major Hodges, October 29, 2018.

23. A Tragic Loss

p. 157: When they sleep at all . . . inside the cave: Author interview with Nikornchai Phopluechai, October 5, 2018; he told me that during the rescue, the SEALs slept inside the cave.

p. 157: Not every Thai Navy SEAL . . . and rushed to Mae Sai: Author interview with Thai Navy SEAL commander Chaiyananta Peeranarong, October 30, 2018.

p. 158: One of the SEALs to come out . . . bring the boys home": Asaree Thaitrakulpanich, "'Sergeant Sam,' Cave Rescue Hero Who Wanted to 'Bring

Boys Home,'" *Khaosod English*, July 6, 2018, http://www.khaosodenglish.com /news/2018/07/06/sgt-sam-cave-rescue-hero-who-wanted-to-bring-boys-home/.

p. 158: Late at night on July 5 . . . tanks along behind them: "Ex-Navy Diver Dies on Oxygen Supply Mission," BBC News, July 6, 2018, https://www.bbc .com/news/world-asia-44734385; Michael Safi and Jacob Goldberg, "Former Thai Navy SEAL Diver Saman Kunan Dies Inside Cave from Lack of Air," *The Guardian*, July 6, 2018, https://www.theguardian.com/world/2018/jul/06 /former-thai-navy-seal-diver-saman-kunan-dies-from-lack-of-air-inside-cave.

p. 158: The SEALs stationed in Chamber 3 . . . almost fifteen hours: "Against the Elements."

p. 158: When Saman's partner . . . Saman behind him: "Ex-Navy Diver Dies on Oxygen Supply Mission," BBC News, July 6, 2018, https://www.bbc.com/news /world-asia-44734385; Michael Safi and Jacob Goldberg, "Former Thai Navy SEAL Diver Saman Kunan Dies Inside Cave from Lack of Air," *The Guardian*, July 6, 2018, https://www.theguardian.com/world/2018/jul/06/former-thai -navy-seal-diver-saman-kunan-dies-from-lack-of-air-inside-cave.

p. 159: The addition of the clunky coils . . . sumps even more dangerous: Author interview with Major Hodges, October 29, 2018. During this interview, Major Hodges said he wondered if Saman could have become tangled in the mess of tubes and cables and died struggling to free himself. There is no defini- tive way to know how Saman drowned, but cave diving is so perilous that any number of factors could have caused his death.

p. 159: The Navy SEALs are like a family . . . the rest of the operation: Author interview with Commander Chaiyananta, October 30, 2018.

24. Risking It All

p. 161: "they'll be bringing out thirteen dead bodies": Author interview with Vern Unsworth, October 5, 2018.

p. 162: "Human Responses to Levels of Oxygen Concentration": Edward Naranjo, "Oxygen Deficiency: The Silent Killer," EGS Today, December 1, 2007, https://www.ehstoday.com/fire_emergencyresponse/ehs_imp_77598.

p. 162: Two days earlier, Governor Narongsak . . . opposite of zero risk: Author interview with Major Hodges, October 29, 2018; "New Video Emerges of Trapped Thai Football Team in Good Spirits," France 24, July 4, 2018, https://www.france24.com/en/20180704-thailand-new-video-football-team-boys-trapped-cave-good-spirits.

pp. 162–163: The Thais are also heartened . . . up to the surface?: Thanet Natisri rescue diary.

p. 163: On the morning of July 6 . . . could wash it all away: Ibid.

p. 163: "If the water levels rise again . . . become impossible: Author interview with Major Hodges, October 29, 2018.

p. 163: The British divers made . . . vacuum-packed meals: Thanet Natisri rescue diary.

pp. 163–164: If the boys are going to wait out . . . a successful drilling operation: Author interview with Major Hodges, October 29, 2018.

pp. 164–165: Thanet speaks to Colonel Singhanat . . . agrees to a brief conversation: Thanet Natisri rescue diary.

p. 166: As the rear admiral listens . . . to support a dive rescue: Author interview with Claus Rasmussen, October 18, 2018; Thanet Natisri rescue diary.

p. 166: He says that in the evening . . . to discuss the path forward: According to Thanet Natisri, there was an impromptu meeting that afternoon with some members of the Thai leadership. The minister of the interior called into the meeting and participated over speakerphone. During this first meeting, it was decided that they would hold a full meeting with all leadership present later that evening, when there could be a more formal presentation of the dive-rescue plan. For brevity's sake, I have chosen to omit this "meeting about a meeting" from the main text.

25. A Very Important Meeting

The decisive meeting that took place on July 6 was top secret. No one was allowed to record video, and the minister of the interior instructed the Thais

present not to leak anything to the media. At this time during the rescue, everyone working on the mission was quite sure that at least some of the boys would die, and no one was eager to go on record recommending a plan that ended with casualties. My description of this meeting comes from my interviews with Thanet Natisri and Major Charles Hodges.

p. 169: There is one man . . . Vern are all absent: Author interview with Vern Unsworth, June 3, 2019. Gary Mitchell represented the UK divers at this meeting.

p. 172: "Tham Luang Dive-Rescue Plan": Divers' names and stations were provided to me by Vern Unsworth and Martin Ellis.

p. 173: the minister is convinced that this is the only way forward . . . a letter to the prime minister of Thailand: Author interview with Thanet Natisri, September 25, 2018. Thailand is a constitutional monarchy, with the king serving a primarily symbolic role as the head of state under rules set forth by the constitution. Citizens elect representatives to the National Assembly, who in turn elect a prime minister. In 2014, Thailand's military seized power of the government in a coup, suspended elections, and installed army general Prayut Chan-o-Cha as prime minister ("Thailand Military Seizes Power in Coup," BBC News, May 22, 2014, https://www.bbc.com/news/world-asia-27517591). As the head of Thailand's government, the prime minister had the official final say over whether to proceed with the dive-rescue plan. But it's my understanding that King Vajiralongkorn was very concerned about the rescue and kept informed of all events.

p. 173: With the ink dry, everything is in place: In my interview with Major Hodges on October 29, 2018, he said he was unclear if they had received official permission to carry out the dive-rescue plan that night from Minister Paochinda or if permission still had to be secured from the prime minister. Either way, preparations began immediately and the prime minister did support the rescue plan.

26. Stage One: Rehearsals

p. 174: Planning the diving portion . . . Rick and John and their comrades: Author interview with Major Hodges, October 29, 2018.

p. 176: The first requirement is to find . . . rushing in and flooding the mask: Lunn.

p. 176: Finding the right mask . . . police escort leading the way: Lunn. The Tech Talk sidebar to Lunn's article, p. 86, describes Bristol Channel Diving's efforts to get full-face masks to Tham Luang. Other accounts of the rescue, including Matt Gutman's *The Boys in the Cave*, listed in the bibliography, state that the four full-face masks ultimately used on the Wild Boars were all provided by the US military. Even if this is the case, Bristol Channel Diving's generosity and quick action exemplify how people all over the world were ready and willing to help out with the rescue operation.

p. 176: Ay and the Get-It-Done . . . skip school to help: Author interview with Chaiyon "Ay" Srisamoot, October 7, 2018.

p. 176: It takes some makeshift . . . get the masks to fit: Lunn.

pp. 176–177: Knowing that panic is a diver's . . . excellent sump diver: "Cave Rescue: The Australian Diving Doctor Who Stayed with the Boys," BBC News, July 11, 2018, https://www.bbc.com/news/world-australia-44789693; Yaron Steinbuch, "Doctor Details 'Frightening' Decision to Sedate Thai Soccer Boys," *New York Post*, July 24, 2018, https://nypost.com/2018/07/24/doctor-details -frightening-decision-to-sedate-thai-soccer-boys/.

p. 177: "Dr. Harris's first thought . . . dive kids out in an anesthetized state": Harris, "Thai Cave Rescue."

p. 177: He sedates children . . . especially great with kids: "Cave Rescue: The Australian Diving Doctor Who Stayed with the Boys," BBC News, July 11, 2018, https://www.bbc.com/news/world-australia-44789693; Yaron Steinbuch, "Doctor Details 'Frightening' Decision to Sedate Thai Soccer Boys," *New York Post*, July 24, 2018, https://nypost.com/2018/07/24/doctor-details-frightening -decision-to-sedate-thai-soccer-boys/.

p. 177: The boys' parents aren't told . . . the boys are medicated: Author interview with Chaiyon "Ay" Srisamoot, October 7, 2018. During our interview, Ay and I discussed the Thai government's decision to keep the sedation part of the rescue quiet. He expressed to me that the concept of sedation was "not normal" and many people in that area would have thought it was strange and scary. In fact, even as the rescue was coming to a close, the prime minister denied that the children were given any sedatives, insisting they had only been given "something to make them not too nervous and panic" ("All 12 Boys, Coach

Brought Out," *Bangkok Post*, July 10, 2018, https://www.bangkokpost.com /news/general/1501006/all-12-boys-coach-brought-out).

p. 178: Major Hodges suggests they use . . . the best possible plan: Author interview with Major Hodges, October 29, 2018.

p. 178: "Once the overall plan is agreed . . . Sergeant Anderson and his squadron: Hope Hodge Seck, "'Expecting Casualties': How Airmen Created the Incredible Thai Cave Rescue Plan," Military.com, September 25, 2018, https:// www.military.com/daily-news/2018/09/25/expecting-casualties-how-airmen -created-incredible-thai-cave-rescue-plan.html; Lara Seligman, "Mission Impossible: Inside the Dramatic Cave Rescue of a Thai Soccer Team," Foreign Policy.com, September 20, 2018, https://foreignpolicy.com/2018/09/20/mission -impossible-inside-the-dramatic-cave-rescue-of-a-thai-soccer-team/.

p. 178: The rescue divers are rehearsing . . . their small bodies underwater: Thai Navy SEAL Facebook post, July 20, 2018, https://www.facebook.com /ThaiSEAL/posts/1663048723818520.

p. 179: "We are in a war against the water": Morgan Winsor, "Thai Cave Rescuers at 'War' Against Water in Race to Evacuate Boys' Soccer Team," ABC News, July 7, 2018, https://abcnews.go.com/International/thai-cave-rescuers -war-water-race-evacuate-boys/story?id = 56424543.

pp. 179, 181: Thanet knows that their water-control . . . can do is hope: Thanet Natisri rescue diary.

p. 180: "Practice Makes Perfect": Leach, 123–135, 144; Joe Spring, "Come Out Alive: Practicing Survival Skills," *Outside* online, November 25, 2009, https:// www.outsideonline.com/1817061/come-out-alive-practicing-survival-skills.

p. 181: Back at Tham Luang . . . roads are cleared: "One Way Out."

p. 181: Even though the rescue team . . . wait on standby: "Out of the Dark," transcript, p. 15.

27. Stage Two: "Today Is D-Day"

Unless otherwise noted, this chapter is based on the two Richard Harris lectures listed in the bibliography. SWAN conference attendees recorded Dr. Harris's presentation there and posted it online, where I was able to view and transcribe it. I also consulted nurse anesthetist Cameron Blok-Andersen, CRNA, who provided detailed information about the drugs used by Dr. Harris, including their side effects and how they are administered.

p. 183: "Today Is D-Day": Governor Narongsak quoted in James Doubek et al., "First Boys Are Rescued from Cave in Thailand," NPR, July 8, 2018, https://www.npr.org/2018/07/08/626986096/operations-begin-to-rescue-thai-boys-from-cave.

pp. 183–184: Dr. Harris has told the Thai SEALs . . . after all the boys are out: "Full News Conference." At this news conference, Coach Ek described how he suggested the order the boys would dive out. It just so happens that the boys who lived farthest away were also some of the biggest boys in the group. I wonder if that was a coincidence: Coach Ek would have known that it would be good for the rescue team to have a successful first day, and that success would be more likely with the bigger, stronger boys. I haven't found any other interviews that reveal that Coach Ek purposefully arranged the selection so that the biggest boys would leave the cave first, but it certainly would have been a clever and tender way to do it.

When I met some of the boys' parents at Wat Doi Wao, they told me some details about the rescue that I had not known before, including the order in which some of the boys were brought out. One of the boys' mothers knew the order in which the first four boys were brought out on July 8, and she knew which boys made up the next two groups. But she did not tell me the exact order of the dive rescues on the second or last day.

p. 185: Once all the drugs are given . . . breathing along the way: Stephen Wright, "US Air Force Rescuer Details High-Risk Thai Cave Mission," Military.com, July 11, 2018, https://www.military.com/daily-news/2018/07/11/us-air-force-rescuer-details-high-risk-thai-cave-mission.html.

p. 185: Jason Mallinson has volunteered to be the first rescue diver: "One Way Out."

p. 187: He has decided to . . . child's weight: Dr. Harris tweeted during the 2018 SWAN trauma conference to answer an attendee's question about dosages used during the rescue: "PO Alprazolam (0.5 mg) and IM ketamine (5mg/kg) with additional half dose en route administered by Thai divers if required. Emphasis was to err on the side of anesthesia. Effective communication proved essential." Dr. Richard Harris (@drharry64), Twitter, July 28, 2018. The tweet has since been deleted.

p. 187: Even then, he expects the drug will wear off after about forty minutes: Harris, "Thai Cave Rescue." During this lecture, Dr. Harris mentions that each boy got two or three top-up doses of ketamine during the three-hour trip out of the cave.

28. Alone in the Dark

Unless otherwise noted, this chapter is constructed from interviews with Jason Mallinson and Chris Jewell included in the ABC *20/20* episode "One Way Out," listed in the bibliography.

p. 190: Danish diving instructor . . . they will attempt to rescue today: Author interview with Claus Rasmussen, October 18, 2018.

pp. 190–193: Together with cave divers Craig Challen . . . waiting is the hardest part: During my interview with Claus Rasmussen on October 18, 2018, he described this experience of getting the first four boys through Chamber 8, including the frightening incident with Night. Dr. Harris also discussed this in Harris, "Extraordinary Cave Rescues and Retrievals."

p. 193: Jason Mallinson is nearly wiped . . . tackle this one section: "Out of the Dark," transcript, pp. 16–17.

p. 194: Aside from practicing on a plastic water bottle . . . never given a shot: This lack of experience administering injections is described in Challen, "Thai Cave Rescue."

p. 194: Sergeant Anderson checks behind him . . . hospital in Chiang Rai: Rosemary E. Lunn, "Thailand Cave Rescue: Dr. Richard Harris Tells His Story," *X-Ray Magazine*, July 13, 2018, https://xray-mag.com/content/thailand-cave-rescue-dr-richard-harris-tells-his-story; Michael Safi, "'We Don't Know How It Worked': The Inside Story of the Thai Cave Rescue," *The Guardian*, July 14, 2018, https://www.theguardian.com/news/2018/jul/14/we-dont-know-how-it-worked-the-inside-story-of-the-thai-cave-rescue.

p. 195: Vern Unsworth stands at his . . . two weeks: Author interview with Vern Unsworth, October 5, 2018.

29. Mission Possible

p. 197: Note is loaded onto the last . . . He's alive: "Against the Elements."

pp. 197, 199: They quickly measure . . . lifted high above the rocky slopes: "One Way Out."

p. 198: This illustration was designed based on information from Hannah Beech et al., "'Still Can't Believe It Worked': The Story of the Thailand Cave Rescue," *New York Times*, July 12, 2018, https://www.nytimes.com/2018/07/12/world /asia/thailand-cave-rescue-seals.html, photos taken by the US Air Force, and "Thai Cave Rescue: How the Boys Were Saved," BBC, July 18, 2018, https:// www.bbc.com/news/world-asia-44695232. In Craig Challen's lecture to the Old Flier's Group, he explains why this image is the most accurate (Challen, "Thai Cave Rescue"). Email correspondence with Rick Stanton on August 30, 2019, provided important details about how the boys were dived out.

p. 199: Vern is stationed at . . . the first Wild Boar go free: Author interview with Vern Unsworth, October 5, 2018.

p. 199: Thanet Natisri is with his team . . . It has: Author interview with Thanet Natisri, September 25, 2018.

pp. 199–200: Down the mountain at Sai Tong . . . thrum of the super-pumps: Author interview with Colonel Singhanat, October 6, 2018.

p. 200: In base camp, Governor Narongsak . . . news to the waiting media: "Against the Elements."

p. 201: When their classmates, who have been glued . . . and shout with joy: Dumrongkiat Mala, "Football Pitch Turns into Ghost Town," *Bangkok Post*, July 10, 2018, https://www.bangkokpost.com/news/general/1500558/football-pitch -turns-into-ghost-town.

p. 201: "After sixteen days, we finally get to see the Wild Boars in the flesh": "Against the Elements."

p. 201: "They did it . . . the first four out": These were my words. I was in Thailand visiting my family between June 23 and July 7, 2018. We flew home to the United States just before the dive rescue began. The first night I hardly slept, checking and rechecking my phone for updates until I knew that the first boys had made it out.

30. The Sleeping Lady Has the Final Say

p. 203: Four members . . . plus three Thai SEALs and Dr. Pak, inside: "Against the Elements."

p. 203: Luckily, the second day . . . take off any gear: "One Way Out." In Harris, "Thai Cave Rescue," Dr. Harris outlines the time the rescues took on each day of the mission.

pp. 203–204: Even though the divers tried to be gentle . . . neoprene to cushion them: Challen, "Thai Cave Rescue."

p. 204: The divers' hands are . . . and infected: Author interview with Vern Unsworth, October 25, 2018; Vern recalled seeing a nasty infection on Rick's hands.

p. 204: They had wanted . . . day of the operation: Author interview with Claus Rasmussen, October 18, 2018.

pp. 205–206: Thanet's team has not . . . The divers are going inside: Thanet Natisri, rescue diary.

p. 206: Vern Unsworth stands at his . . . hopes they don't start now: Author interview with Vern Unsworth, October 5, 2018.

p. 207: Today, the rescue divers . . . all the way out of the cave: "One Way Out." In my email correspondence on September 4, 2018, with Martin Ellis of the BCRC, he told me about Jim Warny diving out the coach on the last day.

p. 207: Coach Ek is first up . . . same treatment as the boys: Harris, "Thai Cave Rescue."

p. 207: "When it's Mark's turn . . . mask doesn't fit": "One Way Out."

pp. 207–208: Jason has a critical decision . . . the last dive rescue of the mission: "One Way Out"; "Thai Cave Survivors Reunited with British Rescue Divers," ITV *This Morning*, October 30, 2018, https://www.youtube.com/watch?v = wTCF wjjaaMg.

p. 208: Closer to the entrance . . . holding Pong under one arm: "One Way Out"; "Thai Cave Rescue: British Diver Lost Rope Guide for Four Minutes during Mission," 5 News, July 18, 2018, https://www.youtube.com/watch?v = FM_0o BhvyAc. Although I learned some of the order of how the boys were brought out by speaking to their parents in Thailand, I learned which boy was carried by Chris Jewell in ABC correspondent Matt Gutman's book *The Boys in the Cave*, listed in the bibliography.

p. 209: Chris hears a voice . . . get him to the finish line: "One Way Out."

p. 209: At 6:47 p.m. . . . is alive and well: "Against the Elements."

pp. 209–210: But the rescue still isn't complete . . . as the water surges up behind them: Author interview with Major Hodges, October 29, 2018; Forester.

p. 210: The rescuers emerge from the cave . . . somehow they succeeded: "Out of the Dark."

p. 210: Major Charles Hodges has avoided . . . the moment starts to sink in: Author interview with Major Hodges, October 29, 2018.

31. It Should Not Have Worked

p. 213: "When the boys wake up . . . relieved and happy": "Exclusive Thai Cave Rescue Interview."

p. 213: all thirteen are in good health: "Thailand Cave Rescue: Boys, Coach Mourn Diver's Death, Observe Minute of Silence in His Honor," FirstPost.com, July 15, 2018, https://www.firstpost.com/world/thailand-cave-rescue-boys-coach -mourn-divers-death-observe-minute-of-silence-in-his-honour-4745351.html.

p. 213: Coach Ek's core temperature . . . threshold for hypothermia: Harris, "Thai Cave Rescue."

p. 213: Thi woke up from his sedation with a fever: According to his mother.

p. 213: Night and several others . . . but that's about it: Harris, "Extraordinary Cave Rescues and Retrievals."

p. 213: None of the boys remember anything about the rescue: The Wild Boars' appearance on the *Ellen DeGeneres Show*, October 15, 2018, https://www.ellen tube.com/video/ellen-talks-to-thai-soccer team-in-their-first-in-studio-interview -since-cave-rescue.html.

p. 214: After a few days, the boys . . . a request for Kentucky Fried Chicken: "Thai Soccer Players Eager to Eat Their Favorite Foods as They Wait to Go Home," CBS News, July 14, 2018, https://www.cbsnews.com/news/thai-cave -rescue-soccer-players-eager-to-eat-their-favorite-foods-as-they-wait-to-go-home -2018-07-14/.

p. 214: While they are still resting . . . World Cup, after all: "Exclusive Thai Cave Rescue Interview."

p. 214: the kids are finally given . . . such good care of them: "One Way Out."

p. 214: The hospital staff gives . . . the Wat Doi Wao: Author interview with Phra Khru Prayut, October 4, 2018.

p. 214: The rest of the team will soon . . . they would never meet him: "Thai Cave Rescue: Boys Are Told of the Death of Former Navy SEAL Diver Saman Gunan," Australian Broadcasting Corporation News, July 15, 2018, https:// www.abc.net.au/news/2018-07-16/thai-cave-rescue-boys-told-of-diver-saman -gunan-death/9997680; "Full News Conference."

pp. 214–215: They decide that all the Buddhist boys . . . Chamber 9 before they were found: Author interview with Phra Khru Prayut, October 4, 2018. Becoming a monk to honor someone who has passed away, or to "make merit" for them, is a common practice in Thailand.

p. 215: With Coach Ek, the boys . . . after they leave the temple: Hannah Ellis-Petersen, "Thai Cave Boys' Heads Shaved Before Ordination Ceremony," *The Guardian*, July 24, 2018, https://www.theguardian.com/news/2018/jul/24 /boys-rescued-from-thai-cave-become-buddhist-novices.

pp. 215–216: On August 6, the boys . . . as soon as possible: Chinnapat Chaimol, "Wild Boars Back to Class in High Spirits," *Bangkok Post,* August 7, 2018, https://www.bangkokpost.com/news/general/1517062/wild-boars-back-to -class-in-high-spirits.

p. 216: On August 8, Coach Ek . . . into the light: "Stateless Boys and Coach Granted Citizenship," *The Guardian*, August 8, 2018, https://www.theguardian .com/world/2018/aug/09/thai-cave-rescue-stateless-boys-and-coach-granted -citizenship; "Thailand," International Observatory on Statelessness: Thailand, http://www.nationalityforall.org/thailand.

p. 217: They have changed on the inside . . . gratitude for small things": Some of the boys' parents told me this when I met them in Thailand.

pp. 217–218: For sure they are never going . . . with them in the darkness: "Full News Conference."

p. 218: They want to finish school . . . I will try my best": "Exclusive Thai Cave Rescue Interview." My father translated Adul's response, and so it differs from the ABC News translation.

BIBLIOGRAPHY

"Against the Elements." Channel News Asia, August 8, 2018. https://www.channelnews asia.com/news/video-on-demand/against-the-elements/against-the-elements-10600394.

Cassaniti, Julia. *Living Buddhism: Mind, Self, and Emotion in a Thai Community*. Ithaca, NY: Cornell University Press, 2015.

Challen, Craig. "Thai Cave Rescue." Lecture, Old Fliers Group, Jandakot, Western Australia, October 15, 2018. https://www.youtube.com/watch?v = IJGfsd8YHOI.

Ellis, Martin. *The Caves of Thailand*. Vol. 2, *Northern Thailand*. Somerset, UK: Shepton Mallet, 2017.

"Exclusive Thai Cave Rescue Interview: Boys' Soccer Team, Coaches on Harrowing Experience." ABC News, August 23, 2018. https://www.youtube.com/watch?v = Jw0 _5UlFwHA.

Exley, Sheck. *Basic Cave Diving: A Blueprint for Survival*. 5th ed. National Speleological Society, 1986.

———. *Caverns Measureless to Man*. St. Louis, MO: Cave Books, 1994.

Farr, Martyn. *The Darkness Beckons: The History and Development of World Cave Diving*. Sheffield, UK: Vertebrate Publishing, 2017.

Forester, Thad. "Episode 59: Inside the Thai Soccer Team Rescue with Major Charles Hodges." *Patriot to the Core* (podcast), August 20, 2018. http://www.thadforester.com /charleshodges/.

"Full News Conference: Thai Cave Rescue Boys Relive 'Moment of Miracle.'" BBC News, July 18, 2018. https://www.youtube.com/watch?v = 62TWYuFn6xM&t = 29s. The Thai government held a large televised press conference with the Wild Boars on July 18, 2018, after they were released from the hospital. An English-translated version was broadcast by the BBC and the *Washington Post*, but I have mostly relied upon my father's translation of the Thai-language version broadcast by Global News.

Gutman, Matt. *The Boys in the Cave: Deep Inside the Impossible Rescue in Thailand*. New York: Harper Collins, 2018.

Harris, Richard. "Extraordinary Cave Rescues and Retrievals." Lecture, SWAN 2018: Trauma, Critical Care, and Emergency Services Conference, Sydney, Australia, July 28, 2018.

———. "Thai Cave Rescue." Video lecture, World Extreme Medicine Conference, Edinburgh, Scotland, November 25, 2018. https://extrememedicineexpo.com/extreme-medicine-video-library/.

Leach, John. *Survival Psychology*. New York: New York University Press, 1994.

Lunn, Rosemary E. "Getting the Boys Out: Tham Luang Cave Rescue." *X-Ray Magazine*, August 27, 2018. https://xray-mag.com/content/getting-boys-out-tham-luang-cave-rescue.

"One Way Out: Thailand Cave Rescue." Episode of 20/20. ABC, July 27, 2018. https://abc.go.com/shows/2020/episode-guide/2018-07/27-072718-one-way-out-thailand-cave-rescue.

"Out of the Dark." Episode of *Four Corners*. Australian Broadcasting Corporation, July 16, 2018. https://www.abc.net.au/4corners/out-of-the-dark/10000580.

"Rescued Thai Soccer Team Holds a News Conference." *Washington Post*, July 18, 2018. https://www.youtube.com/watch?v = ID8VUkkgLEs.

"Rick Stanton Gives Incredible Account of Thai Cave Rescue." ITV News, July 17, 2018. https://www.youtube.com/watch?v = SnXwvyZhm24.

Stone, William, Barbara am Ende, and Monte Paulsen. *Beyond the Deep: The Deadly Descent into the World's Most Treacherous Cave*. New York: Warner Books, 2002.

Swearer, Donald K., Sommai Premchit, and Phaithoon Dokbuakaew. *Sacred Mountains of Northern Thailand and Their Legends*. Chiang Mai, Thailand: Silkworm Books, 2004.

Tabor, James M. *Blind Descent: The Quest to Discover the Deepest Cave on Earth*. New York: Random House, 2010.

"Thai Cave Rescue," Season 2, Episode 9 of *Drain the Oceans*. National Geographic, September 2, 2019.

Thailand Ministry of Culture. *The Tham Luang Cave Rescue: A Global Mission*. Thailand: 2018.

"Thai Soccer Players Eager to Eat Their Favorite Foods as They Wait to Go Home." CBS News, July 14, 2018. https://www.cbsnews.com/news/thai-cave-rescue-soccer-players-eager-to-eat-their-favorite-foods-as-they-wait-to-go-home-2018-07-14/.

Walker, Matthew. *Why We Sleep: Unlocking the Power of Sleep and Dreams*. New York: Scribner, 2017.

IMAGE CREDITS

pp. ii–iii, vi–vii, and viii: Copyright © by Christina Soontornvat

p. 3: Photo by John Peters/Manchester United via Getty Images

p. 6: Copyright © by Christina Soontornvat

p. 8: Copyright © by Thanet Natisri

pp. 10–11 and 12: Copyright © by Christina Soontornvat

p. 14, top: Copyright © by Christina Soontornvat

p. 14, bottom: Copyright © by Nikornchai Phopluechai

p. 20: Copyright © by Sangwut Khammongkhon/Siam Ruam Jai Mae Sai Rescue Organization

p. 22: Copyright © by Christina Soontornvat

pp. 24 and 25: Copyright © by Sangwut Khammongkhon/Siam Ruam Jai Mae Sai Rescue Organization

p. 26: Copyright © by Christina Soontornvat

p. 29: Courtesy of Thomas Hirsch, licensed under CC BY-SA 3.0

pp. 34 and 37: Courtesy of Vernon Unsworth

p. 38: Shutterstock.com/MemoryMan

p. 39: Copyright © by Sangwut Khammongkhon/Siam Ruam Jai Mae Sai Rescue Organization

pp. 40, 41, and 42: Courtesy of Royal Thai Navy SEALs

p. 44: Courtesy of Vernon Unsworth

p. 47: Shutterstock.com/Shutter_fern168

p. 49, top: Pixabay

p. 49, bottom: Courtesy of Jean Krejca

p. 50: Courtesy of Mikko Paasi/Koh Tao Divers

p. 52: Pixabay

p. 55: Shutterstock.com/SantiPhotoSS

p. 56: Shutterstock.com/MemoryMan

p. 58: Courtesy of Nikornchai Phopluechai

p. 60: Courtesy of U.S. Air Force/Captain Jessica Tait

p. 65: Copyright © by Nikornchai Phopluechai

p. 67: Copyright © by Christina Soontornvat

p. 68: Copyright © by Nikornchai Phopluechai

p. 70: Shutterstock.com/Jig Evil

p. 74: Copyright © by Pongmanat Tasiri/EPA-EFE/Shutterstock

p. 75: Courtesy of U.S. Air Force/Captain Jessica Tait

p. 76: Copyright © by Nikornchai Phopluechai

p. 78: Copyright © by Lillian Suwanrumpha/AFP via Getty Images

p. 81: Shutterstock.com/Kumpol Vashiraaskorn

pp. 83, 84, and 85: Copyright © by Christina Soontornvat

p. 88: Copyright © by Linh Pham/Getty Images

p. 91: Copyright © by Nikornchai Phopluechai

pp. 92, 93, 94, and 95: Courtesy of Thanet Natisri

p. 96: Copyright © by Linh Pham/Getty Images

pp. 98, 101, and 102: Courtesy of U.S. Air Force/Captain Jessica Tait

p. 106: Copyright © by Christina Soontornvat

INDEX

Coach Ek (continued)
  citizenship granted to, 216
  discovery by British divers
      and, 129–130
  early years, 80, 84–86
  families not blaming,
      153–154
  leadership in the cave, 18–
      19, 27–28, 32–33, 52–55,
      79, 86–87, 107
  meditation and, 55, 86
  as a novice monk, 80–81
  on sequence of the boys to
      leave the cave, 183–184
  ordination ceremony at Wat
      Doi Wao, 215, 216
  passion for soccer, 85–86
  relationship with team
      members and their
      families, 7, 153–154
  reminding Wild Boars
      members of their
      strength, 86–87
  rescue from cave, 207
  statelessness, 82, 83, 216
  swimming through flooded
      section, 27–28
  volunteering at Wat Doi Wao
      temple, 84–85
  Wild Boar outings and, 2

Denmark, 99
dive rescue
  boys' emotional response to,
      184–185
  divers for, 172, 175–176, 190
  face masks for, 176, 183,
      185, 207
  for first four boys, 184, 189–
      194, 197, 199, 200
  getting support from Thai
      officials for, 164–167,
      169–171, 173
  plan for, 172, 178, 183–185,
      198
  rainfall and, 179, 205–206
  reactions from others during,
      199–201
  reasons for supporting a,
      161, 163–164

rehearsals, 178, 179, 180
  second day of, 203–204
  sedation for, 176–178, 185,
      186–187, 193–194
  Thai leadership's opposition
      to, 162–163, 171
  third day of, 206–211
  water management for, 179,
      181, 205
divers, cave. See cave diving/
    divers
Dom, 3, 5, 51, 184, 203,
    214. See also Wild Boars
    players
donations for rescue operation,
    110, 144
drilling
  into the Nang Non
      mountains, 63, 90, 136,
      173
  at Sai Tong pond, 92, 92–93,
      93, 110
drones, 64, 69
drowning, 45, 99, 158–159

electrical cables, 58, 75, 128,
    155, 208

face masks, 43, 151, 176, 183,
    185, 189, 207–208, 209
family members
  boys writing notes to, 152–
      153, 152–153
  Coach Ek and, 7, 153–154
  feelings of, during rescue
      operations, 97
  first response to missing
      boys, 21
  gathering at mouth of the
      cave, 23–24, 24, 32, 41,
      65, 66, 134
  in hospital after rescue, 213
  knowledge about sedation,
      177
  Kruba Boonchum and,
      68–69, 109
  learning the first four boys
      got out, 200–201
  learning their sons have
      been found, 134, 135

offerings to Sleeping Lady of
    Nang Non, 65–66
  prayers by, 39, 109
  receiving and writing notes
      to boys in the cave,
      152–154, 152–153
  Wild Boar members thinking
      about, 32, 80
farmers, 93–95, 110
Finland, 99
flash flooding, in karst cave
    systems, 29, 74
food
  absence of while trapped in
      the cave, 32, 53, 103–
      104
  bought before trip to cave
      outing, 2, 4
  brought to boys in the cave,
      139–140, 163
  for rescue workers, 144, 145,
      146, 147
  slowly reintroducing to boys,
      139, 144

Get-It-Done Crew, 142, 143–
    147, 145, 146, 147, 176
groundwater, 31, 89, 91–95
guidelines, 46–47, 48, 49,
    98–99, 100, 112, 126–127,
    137, 138, 150, 188, 194,
    204, 208
Gunan, Saman, 158, 158–159,
    159, 161, 162, 164, 190,
    214, 215, 218

hallucinations, 54, 104, 186,
    187
Halong Bay, Vietnam, 29
Harper, Rob, 36, 71, 73–74, 74,
    98, 165
Harris, Richard, 172, 177, 178,
    183, 184–185, 186–187,
    192, 193, 209
Hidden City, Tham Luang
    cave, 16, 18
Hodges, Charles, 60, 61–63,
    64, 69, 74, 98, 110, 155,
    167, 169–170, 171, 178,
    194, 209, 210